YES

A Positive Faith

YES

A Positive Faith

DAVID L. EDWARDS

DARTON·LONGMAN+TODD

First published in 2006 by
Darton, Longman and Todd Ltd
1 Spencer Court
140–142 Wandsworth High Street
London SW18 4JJ

ISBN 0–232–52620–6

A catalogue record for this book is available from the British Library.

Printed and bound in Great Britain by
The Cromwell Press, Trowbridge, Wiltshire

CONTENTS

PREFACE

⌒

I⊤ ᴍᴀʏ ʙᴇ ᴏꜰ interest if I briefly say how I reached conclusions which, if noticed, may be controversial. Although this book is not about Anglicanism as I have experienced it, or about other joys and sorrows in my life, I have been a priest of the Church of England for fifty years, influenced by having been at the school attached to Canterbury Cathedral. Twice I felt it right to serve as a priest full-time instead of developing academic work in history; I was a Fellow of two colleges, in Oxford and Cambridge. And I have no regret, since I have received so much from being on the staffs of great churches: St Martin-in-the-Fields, Westminster Abbey and two cathedrals, one in mainly rural Norfolk and the other in South London. I was also educated by spells as the editor of a theological publishing house, SCM Press, as the Speaker's Chaplain in the House of Commons and as the chairman of Christian Aid, while week by week I wrote for the *Church Times*.

So I have been privileged. But during that time the active membership of the Church of England has halved. This decline is typical of most denominations and most countries in Europe and problems may lie ahead even in regions where churches now grow, because modern education will spread questioning or scepticism. Of course the causes of decline are not all intellectual, and in the churches which are already experiencing this crisis it is often said that the answer is to be more attractive and useful to people and to communicate the unchanging message using up-to-date methods and styles. But I have found myself unable to agree that this is an adequate strategy. The churches are usually not regarded as menaces and being old-fashioned need not be held against them, but it seems to me that the basic question for many people today is whether the churches are speaking the truth. Especially since I have become more of a consumer rather than a producer of church life in my retirement, I have seen ever more clearly how strange must seem the stories and teachings (less polite words would be 'myths' and 'dogmas') which can be taken for granted in official religion. No outreach by the churches will be enough unless their message is reconsidered, and where necessary revised or rephrased, with adequate seriousness and courage, to be accompanied by all their good works. I long to help and have needed help myself, so here I have summed up a faith which did not reach and retain this form easily.

In 1963 I was briefly connected with fame because I published Bishop John Robinson's controversial best-seller *Honest to God*. For a time it seemed that its unusual frankness might arouse 'a new stirring in English Christianity', as I hoped when I edited *The Honest to God Debate*. But in the main I was wrong to hope. In another much-discussed book, *The Death of Christian Britain* (2001), Callum Brown surveyed later history and reached the verdict that 'quite suddenly in 1963 something very profound ruptured the character of the nation and its people, sending organised Christianity on a downward spiral to the margins of social significance.' Although I do not believe that Bishop Robinson's little book started that spiral, I do think that the gradual secularisation of Britain and the rest of Europe, and of much modern life elsewhere, has been 'something very profound', so that I want to move beyond questioning which can be, or seem, destructive. In its twentieth century Christianity faced many enemies and many Christians were killed, but now a form of materialism far more relaxed than Communism or the Nazi creed can be said to be killing faith itself. That challenge calls for positive attempts to state what is now credible.

It is, however, often said that when that challenge is heard responses can be so different that they are tearing the Christian Church apart. As is to be expected, the battleground where the confrontation receives the most attention is morality about sex. In these wars of words, which are beyond question more than games on a playing field, Christians called conservative, orthodox or traditionalist oppose Christians called liberal, radical, modernist or open-minded, but I am one of those whose sympathy is divided. What is often presented as conservatism includes, in my view, much that is untrue, at least if taken in a literal sense, but what is often presented as liberalism is too negative. It rejects what is old, and still often loved, without being able to offer a vibrant religion which will attract, inspire and enthuse many millions whose needs arise out of daily life, not out of much study and reasoning. Beliefs are spread by people more than by arguments, and are carried into hearts through rituals, images and stories. I conclude that formal worship in churches is not going to be changed both drastically and rapidly, and that if changes in doctrine are to be made on any large scale those who advocate them must do so without an insensitive dismissal of cherished traditions. Those who regard themselves as progressive ought to acknowledge that in the short run all that can be hoped for realistic-ally is that some 'liberalism' will be accepted more fully as a valid way of being a Christian today, perhaps before a better tomorrow.

It may be thought that this book is impertinent since it covers a large field about which many who are holier and more learned have written with conclusions different from mine, while in order to be constructive but concise I must seem to be dogmatic in my disagreements with dogmatists. Because I try to write in a plain style, I must seem to be shallow. I accept such rebukes. But in case it is also thought that I do not care what conservatively minded fellow Christians think or value, it seems necessary, although not modest, to bare the fact that this is not my first book, although it must be my last.

In 1958 I wrote *Not Angels but Anglicans* with high hopes, and in 2002 *The Church That Could Be* in some disillusionment. In 2004 the last edition of my *What Anglicans Believe* was a non-controversial introduction, renewed after thirty years of reprinting. *The Cathedrals of Britain* has also gone into many editions, largely I suspect because of its very beautiful photographs. In *Leaders of the Church of England 1828–1944* (1971) I paid tribute to some great men; in three volumes I celebrated the heritage of *Christian England* (1981–84); and in 1997 I covered some 650 printed pages in a global history of *Christianity: The First Two Thousand Years*. But I have tried not to get stuck in the past, as I hope could be seen in books such as *Religion and Change* (1969), *The British Churches Turn to the Future* (1974), an exploration of multiculturalism in *The Futures of Christianity* (1989), and *Christians in a New Europe* (1990). I have entered into respectful dialogues – with the Evangelical leader John Stott in *Essentials* (1988), with radical theologians in *Tradition and Truth* (1989), and with the new *Catechism of the Catholic Church* in *What is Catholicism?* (1994).

I have tried to point to a biblical basis in books such as *A Key to the Old Testament* (1976) and *The Real Jesus* (1992), to help fellow seekers in other books from *God's Cross in Our World* (1963) to *After Death?* (1999), and to share the riches of Christian writers of the past in *John Donne, Man of Flesh and Spirit* (2001), and *Poets and God: Chaucer, Shakespeare, Herbert, Milton, Wordsworth, Coleridge, Blake* (2005).

When I proposed this book to my patient publishers I did not expect it to be so dominated in space and substance by questions about Jesus Christ, but it is surely right that the most important dialogue should be with him. Anyone wishing to study him and his first followers by historians' methods would be helped, as I have been, by Gerhard Theissen and Annette Merz, *The Historical Jesus* (SCM Press, 1998), James D. G. Dunn, *Jesus Remembered* (Eerdmans, 2003) and *The Theology of Paul the Apostle* (T. & T. Clark, 1998), and Alexander J. M. Wedderburn, *A History of the Early Christians* (T. & T. Clark, 2004). Another first-class introduction is Arthur Peacocke's *Paths from Science towards God* (Oneworld, 2001), and *God, Humanity and Cosmos*, ed. Christopher Southgate (Continuum, 2005), is a fuller survey. Modern developments are summed up in the *Cambridge History of Christianity* under the remarkable title *World Christianities* for vols. 8 and 9, c.1815–c.1914 ed. Sheridan Gilley and Brian Stanley, c.1914–c.2000 ed. Hugh McLeod (Cambridge University Press, 2006). Essays on *The Modern Theologians* ed. David Ford (Blackwell, 2005) are also excellent.

This book owes much to many people, but to one my debt is supreme and I dedicate it to my wife Sybil, a beloved conservative with an open mind.

DAVID L. EDWARDS
Epiphany 2006

ONE

CHRISTIAN AGAINST CHRISTIAN?

By the year 2000 in the Christian calendar most Europeans had
ceased to look to the churches either for practical help or for spiritual
guidance. A prospering or improving economy and a democratically
elected government, together with sport and the media, supplied most
of their obvious needs and people would assume that if they were to
listen in a church they would not hear the truth spoken or applied
realistically to life's and death's remaining problems. They would have
the impression that preachers do not have an up-to-date understanding
of human nature or of what goes on in the modern world, and in
particular get sex wrong. They would believe that the Bible is treated
with a simple-minded faith which is out of touch with modern knowledge and questions. They would suspect that churches still use prayers
which assume that God controls everything and favours those who ask
politely. It would seem that it is far more useful to develop one's own
spirituality, if necessary under new guidance. The churches would look
like museums of mythology, mostly admirable as architecture but
no longer necessary even as the setting for a wedding, a funeral or a
welcome to a baby.

In response to this rejection or indifference almost all the churches
have become more distinctly defined and tightly organised communities, more deliberately attached to traditional beliefs and values. They
react against the societies around them where they see darkness – the
collapse of morality and the victory of materialism. In their determined
defence of inherited foundations they can seem to resemble the
American Protestants who were the first to be called fundamentalists,
and they are also not completely unlike the Muslims who now live in
Europe in large numbers but take their inspiration from outside a continent which seems decadent because godless. At the same time many
Europeans who accept neither the dogmatism of the churches nor the
discipline of theocratic Islam find wisdom in ancient sources – in

Buddhist meditation, in Hindu mysticism, in practices such as Yoga, or in the still older religion which Christians have called paganism. All these groups have in common a wish to conserve or recover a spirituality which is essentially not modern, whether they look backwards, upwards or inwards.

There is, however, another group which further complicates the religious situation. These people do not belong to the churches, or believe their teachings, with the traditional commitment and assent. They look around them and are on the whole happy to belong to a modern society and to accept and use the science which is its intellectual foundation. But they regard themselves as Christians in some sense, as 71.8 per cent of the population did in the 2001 census of England and Wales. This may be because they recognise the part that Christianity played in the history of Europe or in their own early years, or because they respect Jesus as the best teacher of moral ideals, or because they have had some religious experience which has meant much to them personally although they see no need to make their relationships with the churches more than semi-detached. Or people who are full of criticisms and doubts may still 'go to church' quite often and 'get something out of it'. And all such people, whether or not they are involved in church life, may be called 'liberal'.

Many of these attitudes have made the conservatively minded suspicious if not hostile. Are liberals now mere parasites, contributing nothing positive? Or are they traitors who work actively to make others share their own half-concealed rejection of Bible and Church, of Christ and God? 'Parasite' comes from the Greek term for a hanger-on who gets a free meal – so are liberals no more than useless pests? Or do they sit brooding like Judas at the last supper? The tension or conflict between conservatives and liberals in the understanding of Christianity is at least as severe as any division between churches after a dispute about the details of traditional orthodoxy. It can seem a battle between Christianities, like a clash between tectonic plates on which continents are built, but in view of the crisis confronting all forms of this faith in Europe, and potentially elsewhere, a better comparison might be with a fight in a rowing boat during a storm.

In abstract terms this controversy can be analysed as a dispute between two theories about what constitutes 'truth'. Philosophers note that many people tend to think that a statement is true if it fits into other statements regarded as reliable. There is an intellectual or cultural system, and the question to ask is 'does this agree with other statements which we believe are true?' But in accordance with a different theory about truth, people can accept a discovery if it is thought to fit into known facts, whether or not it fits neatly into existing beliefs. To them what matters is not the coherence of a closed system but the correspondence of new proposals with existing knowledge. But those are good theories about the differences between the temperaments of individuals – philosophy about psychology. Since individuals are heavily influenced by society, it is also helpful to look at the history of large movements. Conservatism in religion can appeal not only to people who defend their national heritage or their own privileges and power, but also to people who defend freedom against the power of a regime which is evil: so we shall look at Germany as we might have looked at the Soviet Union. Conservatism in religion can be a part of a much wider rejection of modernity and that can appeal to a wide range of people who feel threatened or excluded by modernisation: so we shall look at the Catholics in France and the Evangelicals in the USA. A conservative form of Christianity can be the strongest emotional force in a very large region which is not yet fully modernised: so we shall look at Latin America and southern Africa. But that is not all that can be said about Christianity, the religion with the longest and closest association with modernity, having a membership of one kind or another which now includes almost a third of humankind. At present its most public expression is in churches which are mainly conservative, but Christian liberalism may be seen to have its own place and power, appealing to people who seek a more truthful and realistic way of being a follower of Jesus Christ in a world which is, step by step, escaping from a past of ignorance, poverty and humiliation. One reason why this matters is that after AD 2000 Christianity may have a future ahead of it of two thousand million years, inevitably years of change.

In the history of the defeat of the intellectual kind of liberalism in the churches the clearest and best known development was in Germany, and the disaster began because liberals who look forward to a glorious future can be as mistaken as conservatives who look back to a more glorious past. As the nineteenth century progressed, this country outstripped the rest of Europe both in its economy and in its cultural life. German scholars were the pioneers in the study of the Bible in a spirit which was, or attempted to be, as scientific as any of the new industries. They were the first to discover how the Hebrew Bible had been written and bravely they went back behind Paul and the gospels in the ambition to meet the 'Jesus of history'. Inevitably there was no quick agreement about his real identity. One of the earliest verdicts was that he was a political revolutionary whose corpse had been hidden by his followers. Then a closer study of the New Testament seemed to show that he had relied on a miraculous intervention by God and had died in bitter disillusionment, so that a Christian life such as Albert Schweitzer's had to draw very liberally on other sources of inspiration.

But the main movement in German Protestant theology presented Jesus in a way which was more congenial to the proud Age of Progress. He had been a teacher of the most noble of all visions which have inspired humanity: he had preached the Fatherhood of God, the unique value of each human soul, and the primacy of love in the brotherhood of 'Man' (this Germany was still a place of male supremacy), and he had practised this gospel by loving and healing. Sadly, it was believed that later the Church named after him had become obsessed first by a need to define his uniqueness in terms supplied by Greek philosophy, then by a need to control behaviour by methods supplied by Roman law, and then by the need to meet an unhealthy sense of personal guilt. But in a happier age Jesus could be seen as the advocate and announcer of the progressive government of the world by the Father, with love for all, and that was the essence of Christianity, now rediscovered by progressive Germans under the patronage of the Kaiser and his new empire.

The disaster of this German Liberal Protestantism was that in 1914 it got mixed up with another kind of march into the future, the father-land's invasion of France through neutral Belgium. The pastor of a parish in Switzerland, Karl Barth, was horrified to find the names of his honoured teachers on a list of intellectuals in public support of the war. He rang what he called a church bell. This protest inaugurated 'neo-orthodoxy', essentially a recovery of the vision of the inter-national Church as witness to the supreme authority of the Bible. It could be said that Scripture 'reads us' and does not fail to notice sin in every nation including ancient Israel and modern Germany. Twenty years later Barth had to protest again, this time against the 'German Christianity' which had hailed Hitler almost as the new Messiah. The immediate issue was the Nazis' demand that Christians of Jewish descent should be excluded from all offices in the Church, but behind this was pressure to take everything Jewish out of German Christianity. Protestants who agreed with Barth's protest formed the Confessing Church as a minority whose most famous teacher was Dietrich Bonhoeffer. He held that 'when Christ calls a man he bids him come and die', and he did die, a martyr regarded as a traitor because involved in a plot to assassinate the Führer. He was not completely a disciple of Barth, but he certainly agreed with Barth's central message that Christianity needs a backbone if it is to confront evil – a backbone not provided by liberalism.

When Germany underwent another experience of defeat and depres-sion, the most influential Protestant theologian was Rudolf Bultmann, but he did not put the historical Jesus at the centre; as a New Testament scholar he thought that very little could be said truthfully about that far-off figure. But an appeal could be made to the fact that Jesus was crucified, and that was all-important. The cross challenged Germans to decide whether or not his death was a total defeat like theirs – or is it for ever God's strange victory which can be shared as faith arises? This was a coldly sober and painfully reduced version of Liberal Protestantism but like the optimistic version of the early 1910s it had its hour and became obsolete as the situation changed. The Communist regime in East Germany collapsed and in the West, and gradually in the East also, consumerism with long holidays was now what gave human existence meaning. In prison alongside enemies of the Nazis whose motivation had not been primarily religious, Bonhoeffer had wondered whether when Germany recovered from its self-inflicted tragedies, it would have grown out of 'religion' in its old shapes – and this could now seem to have happened. But what Bonhoeffer had not expected also happened: after the enthusiasm in the 1960s for a new start in a new society, many Protestants rediscovered the value of a Bible-based tradition as a source of distinctiveness and strength under pressure.

In the Catholic half of western Europe the Church has almost always condemned 'liberalism'. The word was first used prominently in the 1820s when some French priests saw the future as lying with democracy and hoped that a pope would place himself at the head of that advancing cause. But this was a period when popes still accepted slavery, attacked medical developments such as vaccination, resisted religious liberty for non-Catholics in mainly Catholic countries, and conducted the government of the Papal States in Italy in a spirit far from democratic. Fearful of what might happen if they showed weakness they allied themselves with other monarchs, and after seeing this the leading pro-democracy clergy in France dissociated themselves from their conservative church, even in matters of religion. In 1864 Pius IX issued his defiant *Syllabus of Errors*, one error being the idea that 'the Roman pontiff can, and ought to, reconcile and adjust himself to progress, liberalism and modern society'. Six years later the First Vatican Council declared any pope 'infallible when in the discharge of his office as the pastor and teacher of all Christians he defines a doctrine regarding faith or morals to be held by the Universal Church'.

As that council dispersed without concluding its business the Italian national army entered Rome and the Pope became 'the prisoner in the Vatican', not recognising the newly victorious state. But against the expectation of Pope Pius, he and his successors became the sovereigns not only of Vatican City but also of a worldwide, and very Roman, Catholicism. This grew much larger in numbers and much deeper in devotion, and was unmistakably conservative in doctrine. When another French priest, Alfred Loisy, urged that German biblical scholarship could be accepted along with Catholic spirituality, his suggestion was that Jesus had expected the kingdom of God but the Church had been given instead. However, he was denounced as a 'modernist', and an anti-modernist oath was imposed on all who claimed to teach the Faith. Modernising France became more 'liberal' in the sense that Catholics were no longer allowed to indoctrinate the nation's children in the nation's schools, and in 1905 the state ceased to pay the clergy and broke any other formal connection with the Church. But in France conservative Catholics who wished to be fully faithful now looked to Rome, not Paris, and around the world millions looked in the same direction. For one example, Irish Catholics, already accustomed to prefer the Church to colonial rule by British Protestants, became all the more loyal to Rome when forced to emigrate by otherwise inescapable poverty or by famine. And patriotic Poles retained their identity through the Church in resistance to Protestant Prussia and Orthodox Russia.

In the history of Christianity power had often been linked with masculinity. The wrath of the Almighty Father had been feared, the courage of the Son and Word had won followers, the leaders had all been men, and the union of the sexes had been thought inferior to celibacy. Catholics had believed that the 'original sin' of Adam was transmitted by lust in the conception of every child. Now, in the nineteenth century, warnings about hell continued but so did the fact that the Church's most active members were women, often grateful for spiritual strength in a humble life of obedient work for men and children. Such encouragement was reinforced by a new emphasis on the Catholic home and the parish school, on a more kindly image of the Father, on the love radiating from the 'sacred heart' of Jesus, and on new definitions of beliefs about his deeply loved mother. In 1854 Pius IX taught formally that the Virgin Mary was 'from the moment of her conception . . . kept free from all stain of original sin' (her Immaculate Conception), and in 1950 Pius XII made it a vital part of the Faith that she, 'having completed her earthly life, was in body and soul assumed into heavenly glory' (her Assumption). Up to a point the Church was feminised.

In the 1960s 'liberalism' and 'modernism' remained dead for faithful Catholics, but in the unexpected Second Vatican Council the bishops did not define new dogmas. Instead they threw the Church's windows open, looked at the world without total condemnation, and breathed some fresh air. Democracy and religious liberty were embraced; the Church was seen as a people moving through history on pilgrimage, not as a rule-bound institution, and the Eucharist was an action shared by the baptised and using their usual language; the Bible was seen as the originating source of all the Church's tradition; the baptised in other churches were greeted as being in some sense within the Church of Christ; other religions were recognised as being in some important ways witnesses to the truth; all the world's peoples were invited to accept the Church as their ally in seeking justice and peace. Even liberals could accept – while interpreting – this council's definition of biblical authority: 'the books of Scripture teach firmly, faithfully and without error that truth which for the sake of our salvation God wished to see confided' to them. The spirit of the council was registered on the face of the pope identified with it, John XXIII: this stout conservative smiled.

But the 1960s were followed by different years in the Catholic Church. Thousands of priests chose to leave and marry, millions of the laity chose to use artificial contraception and a new pope responsible for upholding tradition grew depressed. Then under John Paul II the papacy was again substantially reinvented as a confident, decision-making institution close to the public in at least some senses: the pope taught fluently, travelled internationally, was often on TV and knew how to command and delight a crowd. He dedicated an unusually long pontificate to the preaching of a message inspired (as he believed) supernaturally but based in part on his own tough experience of life in Poland, with the Church at the heart of survival under Nazis and Communists. He was convinced that a largely traditional form of Catholicism could and should be communicated more vigorously to the world of today and should now be identified with the defence of human rights to liberty, spiritual growth and the basic necessities of physical life, 'life' being from conception to a natural death. He played a major role in the defeat of Communism in Eastern Europe and did what he could to have a similar impact on consumerism in the capitalist West. To undergird this firm gospel by discipline and unity in the Church, canon law was slightly revised in a new code, and so was doctrine in a new 'Universal Catechism' and actions against individuals around the Catholic world made it clear that radically new thinking about theology or ethics was not wanted. This restoration of conservatism was further strengthened by the election of Benedict XVI in 2005. He had become sternly anti-liberal when shocked by what he saw as anarchy in the 1960s, in his native Germany and even in the Church.

New ideas have never been welcomed rapidly in the Orthodox Churches of the East, whose claim has been to be more traditional than the innovating Catholics of the West. For them, doctrine and liturgy were shaped in the fourth and fifth centuries, and although the Byzantine empire was overwhelmed by Islam, new centuries brought new incentives to be strictly conservative: in Russia the Church was kept out of politics and cultural life by the iron control of the Tsarist state and by the peasants' simple devotion, and in the Balkans the Church conserved national identities against Turkish rule. The twentieth century brought persecution in the Soviet Union, much suffering in the Balkans, and unsettlement in the Orthodox who had migrated to America or Australia – and did not bring any strong temptation to alter the Faith, or the Liturgy, or the ancient organisation under the Patriarchates of Constantinople, Alexandria and Antioch, or the practice of self-government in national (and nationalist) churches. So there has been no Orthodox equivalent of the Second Vatican Council. Orthodoxy, it seems, is to stand or fall by its faithfulness to a tradition which has quietly given spiritual food to millions who through the worship have glimpsed heaven and felt the power of holiness – and which has often been at the heart of a community under threat.

The story of Protestantism in the USA has not been entirely different from its history in Germany. There too the nineteenth century brought optimism about progress and the human, historical figure of Jesus seemed to inspire or confirm many hopes – even hopes that progress would be such that without any radical break in history Christ would return to reign for a thousand years. But there scholars were not so important. The men and some women who mattered were preachers who, having taken their churches into the migration to the West, and having put idealism into the defeat of the slave-owning states of the South, led a mission offering both religious salvation and social betterment as an industrialising nation became harshly urbanised. In this crusade divisions between Christians were not so sharp as they were to become. The South remained more conservative than the North, but slavery no longer caused battles. In the North more liberal churches prospered because without much controversy they applied ethics inspired by the Bible to daily life. Protestants of every kind together secured the prohibition of the manufacture and sale of alcohol (1920–33). And the Catholicism of the new immigrants proved to be so thoroughly at home in 'Christian America' that the Vatican had to warn against 'Americanism'.

American Christianity remained relatively united against new enemies: the depression of the economy from 1929, the war against the Nazis and the Japanese, the cold war against Communism. In 1914 a series of booklets defending traditional doctrines had earned for this theological reaction the nickname 'fundamentalism', but in 1925 an attempt to ban the teaching of evolution from the nation's schools had ended in ridicule, so that the 'battle for the Bible' had not been very loud. It had helped that many liberals had moved away from the isolationist pacifism and the excessive optimism of earlier years, so that the new 'realism' of Reinhold Niebuhr was not very distant from the tough neo-orthodoxy of Karl Barth. 'Christian America' could, it seemed, still combine in crusades which ended in victories. No one in Congress voted against the addition of 'In God We Trust' to the coinage in 1954. But many things changed when a black woman refused to give up her seat on a bus in 1955. The consequent crusade against racial segregation had triumphed before the murder of its prophet, Martin Luther King, and one of its triumphs was to discredit the religion which had supported racism after slavery in the South, a mixture of the Bible used selectively to justify white supremacy, with otherworldliness to console black subordination. Conservatism of that sort was roundly defeated. But a conservatism which had largely shed racism was far more successful when it crusaded in order to overturn other victories won by a liberalism which campaigned not only for the 'civil rights' of blacks but also for the 'civil liberties' of whites who rejected conservative morality.

Biblical teachings, and even prayer, were prohibited in the nation's schools: the American innovation separating Church and State had been intended to remove the state's support and control from any denomination, but now the state seemed to be removing the Bible's God from the American future. The new affluence left spiritual needs unmet; the new morality aborted babies in the womb and spread sexual diseases headed by AIDS; divorce was an epidemic killing families, and so was the encouragement of mothers to work outside the home; the new terrorism, using the rhetoric of a non-Christian religion, brought mass murder to New York; and provocative homosexuals were destroying the most basic of all distinctions, between men and women. A proposal for a symbolic change in the law provided a new battleground as men and women were summoned to fight the idea that such partnerships, now often called gay marriages, must be accepted by the public and registered by the government.

Conservative congregations were now the ones which grew as the liberals had grown in the 1920s, partly because of businesslike efficiency but mainly because of the wish to 'take my nation back' from liberalism. By the 1980s a large part of the Evangelical sub-culture, now allied with conservative Catholics, had become militantly political and had mastered the skills needed to apply pressure in a democracy. Successive presidents owed some of their support to hopes that they would sweep back the tide of liberalism, and as the twentieth century became the twenty-first, a Methodist converted from an alcoholic and life-wasting past twice won the White House.

The Evangelical part of that politically victorious Religious Right was also part of a vigorous international movement, often encouraged by examples of faithfulness and success in the USA. This took more than one shape as it expanded, but one feature common to all Evangelicals was a rejection of a coldly critical approach to the Bible. 'Liberalism' was seen as negative in its motives and results while an enthusiastic faith of 'Bible-believers' could be blessed by success – and visibly had been, in the world's most modern country.

In Latin America the 'liberals' have not been noted for their theological views. But they have been anticlerical – in Mexico, to the extent of a prolonged persecution of the Church (1917–37) – because they have been determined to break the power of bishops appointed first by the colonial governments and then by the Vatican. They saw these bishops as presiding over a Church heavily subsidised out of taxes and favoured in legislation without being able to recruit enough local clergy. At varying speeds from the 1820s the end of colonialism has therefore been followed by the separation of Church and State in the different nations, usually while retaining Catholicism less formally as the 'official' religion.

But the anticlerical liberals did not really win, for they had no real interest in the progress of the people as a whole. The gap between rich and poor remained very wide and under the pressure of discontent many governments became Fascist. Bishops could be found to bless them but, more importantly, the awareness grew in the Church that if only it could reach the people it might inspire a true democracy. From the 1860s thousands of priests and nuns came as missionaries from Europe.

With the 1960s came the Second Vatican Council, which the bishops attended without understanding much of what went on. It had a large impact on their work when they got home. They saw then that they had to reach the people, now mainly in cities and towns and deriving much of their practical religion from Amerindian or African sources. There was a drive to get Catholics studying the Bible and working out its relevance for spirituality and for life in a society with great areas of poverty. And there were solid results: for example, by 2000 the number of priests, almost all born locally, had dramatically increased.

There have been some developments which have made the Vatican, and bishops appointed by it, uneasy. The religious awakening of the laity produced not only an army of catechists and a fleet of sisters but also 'base' communities for study, discussion and co-operation which could not be controlled as the movement called 'Catholic Action' had been. 'Liberation' theologians who denounced the contrasts between rich and poor could be accused of using Marxist categories. And filling gaps left by the continuing shortage of priests in a multiplying population, Protestant preachers evoked 'Pentecostal' experiences of release from low self-esteem and carefully respectful language, in an explosion of enthusiasm gathering many new congregations. But in no case has much attention been paid to unorthodox theology or to history-based criticism of the Bible. The Catholic liberation theologians have been rebels but not heretics, and the Protestant Pentecostalists have been keen to bring the Bible as it is into the hearts of the people. And amid all the changes brought by modernisation, it is estimated that in Latin America about 90 per cent still believe in God.

Worldwide, the numbers of Christians who could be called Pentecostal, or Charismatic while remaining in the historic churches, had probably gown by 2000 to about 500 million (a tenth of them in Latin America). They all testify to intense experiences of the Holy Spirit in addition to the conversion to Christ and the submission to Scripture which are the Evangelicals' essentials. And like most Evangelicals, they would be distressed to be called 'liberal'.

In the Middle East (as in Latin America) membership of an historic church has been hereditary for the most part, but here the vitality of Islam has caused almost all the churches to shrink numerically. The situation is very different in Africa south of the Sahara. There also Islam is a challenge but it can be countered by churches either proud to join almost a thousand million Roman Catholics in other continents or proud to be based on a Bible believed to be more authoritative than the Qur'an. The need has been seen to make Christian worship as full of excitement, power and joy as has been the worship in Africa's own traditional religions, where beliefs were sung and danced, not written, and bodies as well as souls were healed. The result has been that southern Africa is rapidly becoming the new Christendom. European or North American liberalism has seemed irrelevant, not only white in its skin colour but also pale in its faith and feeble in its morality.

The amazing growth of the African churches during the twentieth century (in 1965–2000 from about 75 to about 350 million) owed its initial impetus to foreign missionaries, but these were almost all conservatively motivated (why else would they have left their own lands?) and the large-scale evangelism has been done by Africans with little or no attention to any theological debate in Europe. In Asia too the twentieth-century growth was initiated by foreign missionaries, but there was more bitterness about their links with political or economic imperialism. So in comparison with the size of the populations, the growth has been large only in the Philippines and South Korea, where the churches became 'native' with relative speed. In India and the Buddhist countries converts have come mainly from classes and tribes which had no liking for the religiously based structures of the main society, and consequently there has not been much soul-searching conservation which would have been the Asian equivalent of the liberal dialogue with Western modernity.

In China the Christians grew in courage and numbers after the expulsion of all foreign missionaries in the late 1940s, but here too any dialogue with the dominant ideology, in this case Marxism, has been very difficult. Christians find themselves excluded from the potential sources of influential criticism – the media and the universities. Equally faithful Protestants and Catholics are divided about whether to register their congregations with the government, accepting some control. Those who refuse are closer to the Western category of 'conservative' but neither group is able to maintain many contacts with the rest of the Christian world. Their concern is with their own country and with the survival and quiet growth of its Christian minority, now beginning to confront consumerism, the ideology of the economic growth which Marxism had been unable to inspire.

Those are glimpses of the strength of conservatism in the churches which have now entered Christianity's third millennium. But if we look more closely we can see that the questions and hopes which have been identified with liberalism have not lost all their significance.

The back-to-the-Bible movement among Protestants has had only a limited success in Europe. The great Reformers of the sixteenth century, and the great preachers of the later Evangelical revivals, could count on the possibility that the Bible might be accepted as authoritative by people who therefore might pay attention to a gospel addressed to a sense of personal sin and guilt, but certainly after the 1960s none of these factors could be regarded as prominent in the field – or was it a desert? – to be addressed in evangelism. There was nothing left to revive. It had to be accepted that people outside the reduced churches would have sharp questions to ask about the Bible and have hopes of material progress rather than of religious salvation. Moreover, the days had passed (almost everywhere) when Protestantism could be supported as a nation's defence against Roman Catholicism. Now Protestants and Catholics came closer together as the Christian minority.

It turned out, however, that the Christian Bible's message could be applied creatively to the evils which in 1939 seemed to be prevailing over the whole of Europe – and applied in a way which could be called 'liberal' because it took the realities of contemporary society with seriousness and sympathy. The struggles against Communists, Nazis and Fascists had been confusing and testing. It had been hard to know when, and how, to resist instead of collaborating, as most German Protestants did with Hitlerism and most Spanish Catholics did with Francoism, and most Christians had expected the future of Communism to be long. But out of these struggles emerged a common vision of Europe's future.

This stressed peace and co-operation between nations, the recognition of extensive human rights and of human spiritual instincts, and a major role for a democratically elected government in the improvement of life for the people. During the great wars these values had inspired courage in dark years and had often been called 'Christian'. Accordingly, when peace came the political parties mainly responsible for the creation of what was to become the European Union identified themselves as Christian Democrats, with a leadership mainly but not exclusively Catholic, a membership not exclusively Christian, and no control by the clergy. These characteristics could be called 'liberal' because political salvation was not now seen to lie either in an almighty state or in the power of an elite. Or it could be 'pluralist' because freedom was now given to almost every group in society, or 'humanist' because the criterion was now human welfare. At first it was supported more on the Right than on the Left, but it was not conservative.

Inevitably many churches, especially those which had been cut off from the West during the years under Communism, have had difficulties in accepting the new goals for society and the new directions for church life. In particular the Roman Catholic Church has been troubled. Popes have preached that in politics 'subsidiarity' is right, with decisions taken at the lowest suitable level, but have strongly denied that the Church is meant to be a democracy or to welcome a free debate about its positions in theology or ethics. In the Church much conversation occurs but no one in authority is obliged to consult – let alone agree with anyone lower in the hierarchy.

The Church has acknowledged the new status of women in many countries, yet women are not included in its own leadership and John Paul II prohibited even the discussion of the possibility of women priests. In practice the Church has also accepted the reality that many millions of Catholics plan their families by using artificial contraception, yet Paul VI refused to accept the advice of an official commission to allow this in doctrine. It has also expressed great anxiety about the shortage of priests which denies the sacraments and pastoral care to the laity, yet compulsory celibacy remains the discipline for priests, with some exceptions made somewhat illogically. Consequently by 2000 the Church's leadership had been placed in nightmarish situations. The practice of regular confession of sins to a priest, regarded for many centuries as the main working key to holiness, had broken down in many regions. Many thousands of adults and children had died because Catholics had persisted in unprotected sex despite the danger of AIDS. Thousands of priests who were not necessarily homosexuals in the exclusive orientation of their sexuality had been convicted of abuse of boys entrusted to their care, and many bishops had been rebuked by the faithful for laxity in response. The fines imposed by courts when these scandals came to light had added severe financial damage to the anger in public opinion.

To many Catholics – as to many others – it is a tragedy that the Church's leadership seems irrevocably committed to positions about gender and sexuality which are nowhere near the centre of the teaching of Jesus or of the consciences of the bulk of the laity. Yet these doctrines are taught as the 'objective norms of morality' derived from 'God's eternal law' as this is reflected in 'natural law'. Seldom has the vulnerability of an impressive belief-system when times change been illustrated more dramatically.

Another disappointment for conservatives has been caused by the vulnerability of the largest of the Orthodox Churches, in Russia. After the collapse of Communism there was admiration for this church's survival under persecution and a willingness to treat it as the carrier of continuity as a nation. Cathedrals and monasteries were restored and bishops were honoured by the leaders of the new state, but there has not been the massive return of the people to the unchanging Liturgy that had been hoped for, since most visitors could not understand what was going on in the long services. In Greece and Serbia liberation from Communism and Fascism has been followed by a modernisation in which the once-loved clergy have seemed wide open to criticism. And in a time when millions of the Orthodox live outside Europe, these minorities have felt great tensions between their participation in the surrounding society and their ethnic loyalty to a Church whose centre seems distant both in space and in time.

The Evangelical movement has never been controlled from a centre such as Rome, or by a very long tradition such as Orthodoxy, and those who belong to it support different denominations and political parties. There is more room for variety and some Evangelicals may be called not 'liberal' but 'open'. These are open-minded about some contemporary developments such as the changed position of women, and they can use discussion in small groups rather than authoritarian and perhaps manipulative preaching. And within the USA as elsewhere, some can be boldly open in their criticism of policies supported by most of their fellow Evangelicals but condemned by what is virtually a consensus in the Christian world outside the USA. While vigorously campaigning against abortion American Evangelicals on the Right have been less concerned about the deaths which have been, or would be, inflicted by their country's massive army and armoury. They have been slow (at least) to trouble their consciences about the stockpile of nuclear weapons, the wars in Vietnam and Iraq, and the plight of the Palestinians. While anxious about the nation's sexual morals, they have been less worried by the fact that the USA is not a good place in which to be vulnerable because young or old, or sick and poor, or in the way when someone decides to use a gun. Often it is still not a good place in which to be black. They have shown little understanding of the reasons why, after a long period when the USA had great prestige, around the world it is now often hated. They have not argued at all strongly for justice, let alone generosity, in trade or aid which could transform the prospects of nations now struggling to survive, and they have taken little interest in American governments' refusals to share international agreements to protect human rights everywhere, to punish war crimes and to control the destruction of nature. On these questions more liberal churches and more 'open' Evangelicals can seem more truly Bible-based.

In Latin America neither Catholic nor Pentecostal vitality has found a complete answer to that continent's spiritual needs. The Catholic bishops all owe loyalty as well as their appointments to the distant Vatican, and under its instructions most have become timid or hostile towards experiments which could have been allowed to become more creative in a society becoming ever more democratic. The Pentecostal preachers, having presided over excitements, have quite often proved unable to retain converts in regular membership because their message has been too simplistic and enthusiasm over a novelty may be followed by boredom with a routine. Also, it has been too individualistic. Unquestionably it has met a spiritual or psychological need but the need met by Latin America's liberation theologians who have concentrated on social problems has been, and is, at least as great. This may be seen in their worldwide influence. They set an example for other prophetic protests – for the affirmation of the rights of the poor in other continents, of women the world over, of people with a physical or mental disability, of people who cannot marry, of endangered species, of the endangered planet.

Throughout the southern hemisphere other creative reactions by Christians will be needed in the future. One demand is bound to be that European and North American influence, in any style, must be reduced drastically. Foreign missionaries are not needed, or welcomed, to the old extent; on the contrary, it is widely felt that 'the West' needs to be taught by 'the rest'. In Africa the proliferation of new churches owing as little as possible to foreign churches, and as much as possible to Africa's own long religious history, has been a phenomenon. Asian spirituality is widely admired and even envied in the secularised West, and is inevitably practised by many Asian Christians even if only in private, so that the time is probably beginning to come when all of Asia's own churches will be more thoroughly and officially Asian, at home in their own immense continent as the churches have been in Europe or the Americas. Already active Christians in the rest of the world outnumber those in Europe and North America. In history the centre of organised Christianity moved to the west and the north; now it is moving south. 'Liberalism' in the old, white style will not be needed, but liberation will be.

In the continents of the Christian future, especially in Africa, the churches need to meet not only the challenge of the religious cultures surrounding them but also the challenge of their societies, where millions upon millions of the children of God are still living in dehumanising poverty and still having many children (in Africa the average age is under fifteen). That does not need to be said to these churches, however: it is already cried out within them. When new Christians still live, or want to live, in a traditional style they often concentrate on the new spiritual power to gain freedom from hostile spirits or disapproving ancestors, but when they have seen the modern world, often from a slum in or around a city, they almost always want a share in it and (unlike Europeans) they may value Christianity as being modern.

One key to a better future is government which is incorrupt and efficient in the service of the people. The churches are, or could be, a significant force in the 'civil society' which supplies ideas, voters and politicians to a democracy. They urgently need to encourage free discussion about local and national problems and the experience of liberals who have done just that in older democracies ought to be relevant although not decisive. Above all, the churches' own style cannot safely remain authoritarian. Bishops may behave like chiefs and preachers like princes but already they depend on the people's support, including financial support and doing most of a church's work, and these are seeds of new forms of active democracy. Courageous protests against the politicians in power have won the world's admiration, but positive models of what it means to be a community where the leaders are responsible to the led are needed even more.

Another key is already firmly in the hands of the churches themselves. Despite limited resources, it is already seen that Christians need to be involved in more than worship, pastoral care and person-to-person evangelism. A share in health education, for example, is part of the necessary mission whatever taboos have to be broken. Male supremacy has to be ended, not least because male promiscuity has been the main cause of the AIDS pandemic. In liberation from poverty, technical training for workshops, or the teaching of more productive agriculture, is not much less Christian than a Bible class. A pump bringing clean water to a village matters almost equally with a church as a sign pointing to the kingdom of God. These projects are essentially self-help but other governments, and international charities, have the privilege of offering aid and in them all there must be an element of international science, which has to be learned. Much has already been done and it is reckoned that across Africa (for example) half of all education, health care and community building is delivered to the people by faith-based groups, but more is already known to be urgent: about 'development' churches, peoples and governments agree.

In the escape from poverty, education, including education in science-based technology, is generally agreed to be the most effective key: its presence is the secret of the rapidly increasing economic liberation of Asia, as its comparative absence is the secret of the poverty of Latin America in comparison with the USA and Canada. Progress means more people learning and using facts. This directly raises the liberal questions about the truth of religious traditions. If education amounts to more than a school or college where the local scriptures are read, recited and obeyed, the result will be that the local religion will be questioned simply because the pupil has been encouraged to think. Traditions about morality, especially in sex and marriage, may seem permanent but it will no longer be taken for granted that they deserve to be obeyed. The fuse will be lit although the explosion of free thought may be delayed. Already the attitudes of the more educated and prosperous in developing countries have become remarkably like the attitudes of the middle classes where, for better or worse, the economy is developed, and already migrants from poorer to richer societies see their children being changed in a process which may be halting and painful but is irreversible.

The Christian Church is often itself a carrier of modernity, however unintentionally. Wherever the Bible is taken, there comes literacy. Wherever international medicine is offered, there comes science. Wherever a new religious opinion is introduced into a traditional society, there comes unsettlement. And wherever the Bible is read in a modern way the possibility arises that the whole structure of a traditional society may be changed by the liberating impact of the Bible's central message. It is significant that so many in the early leadership of post-colonial Africa had been educated in schools and colleges associated with Christian missions, and that so much of the moral leadership in the overthrow of apartheid in South Africa in the 1990s came from

Christians who had to find profoundly religious reasons why the Afrikaaners were wrong to quote the Bible in a conservative defence of the kingdom of the white man.

It is, however, not difficult to understand why Christian liberalism has been so largely defeated or ignored in the world's churches. It has seemed wishy-washy in contrast with the faith of baptised converts. In the experience of many millions the Bible still speaks and commands. During sixteen hundred years most Christians have accepted the 'Nicene' creed as a symbol of their unity in faith and have not contemplated the revision or replacement of the orthodoxy set forth in that agreement. But 'faith' has meant more than assent to written and officially endorsed doctrines. Faith has meant belief in the power of the eternal God through the Lord and Saviour who is enthroned in eternity but also powerfully active in the Church, however 'Church' is understood. It has meant a response to a summons by Christ as a human voice from eternity calling to commitment, discipleship and the new life of a transformed convert. It has meant an invitation to join the saints in the prayer and love which made them saints. It has meant having access at any time of need to the beauty, peace, power and love of God.

There have also been mystics who, often after periods of suffering or uncertainty, have felt closeness to, even union with, God in Christ in a silence greater than words – and Christians who have not been mystics have felt the power of God as Holy Spirit, often in an inrush of energy somewhat like electricity and often as a light showing the way ahead when the world gets very dark. The twentieth century saw the release of uninhibited emotions of certainty, joy and healing in two such Protestant movements, the Pentecostal revival at the beginning of the century and the inter-church Charismatic explosion towards its end. And within the stronger disciplines of Catholicism and Orthodoxy other Christians have had such spiritual power and courage that the twentieth century saw many more martyrdoms than any earlier age. All this can be called 'conservatism' if we remember that this has never excluded some development.

Another explanation of the victories of Christian conservatism can be found in the character of a local church. This is often an extended family, large or small. Here is a fixed point from which to view the world and enter it with a sense of direction. If the Christian fellowship meets in the midst of a non-Christian society it presents an alternative either to that society's own traditions or to the end of the stability of a village. If it meets in a modern society which may be 'Christian' in some sense it offers a deeply appreciated common life in a community where natural communities including families have often broken down or been severely damaged. And if it gathers Christians whose ethnic roots are in another country, it can function very successfully as a support-group.

Typically, people go to church for encouragement and are in no mood for academic arguments about the Bible: they want the Bible to feed them and as the Bible is presented (in the hymns perhaps more than in the sermon) there is a welcome relief from uncertainties and innovations. In the beauty and dignity experienced here (as perhaps nowhere else) a holiday can be taken from the argumentative, the trivial and the sordid. Paradoxically, the new movement of thought which is most likely to appeal to conservatives is postmodernism, which advocates diversity – for it can encourage conservatives to stay more or less as they are, conserving what is sacred.

'Liberalism' does not have that appeal to the heart. But what is it? The easiest answer would be to say that in reality the 'ism' does not exist: there are only argumentative liberals, whose causes are various and whose own minds are often divided. But the Oxford Dictionary lists opinions which have been called by this name and connections between these can be discerned.

The English word comes from the Latin *liberalis* meaning someone not a slave. 'The liberal arts' is an expression not often used nowadays to cover literature, music and the arts, but it refers to activities which can delight people who have some freedom from drudgery. They are, or have been, a privileged elite but 'liberal' can refer to any open-hearted, open-minded person who is free from ignorance or prejudice and who wishes to see the numbers of the privileged enlarged. Such people can be the forerunners followed by great movements seeking the liberation of humankind.

A 'liberal' helping of food can mean 'generous'. In politics it can mean support for change which through the advance of democracy will gradually spread justice, freedom, dignity and opportunity. That can sound like a slogan of the Left, but the word can also signify that the problem of how to attain economic progress is being tackled realistically, for in economics 'liberalisation' can mean the removal of barriers to free competition between businesses and free trade between nations. Wealth in all nations will come when the market, not the state, makes the decisions, for in the market consumers want to buy from whoever has the lowest price and producers are compelled to be efficient in supplying the goods wanted, so everyone gains. Or at least that was the hope in the nineteenth century and many millions previously poverty-stricken did benefit. But in the next century most liberals joined those who

acknowledged a large role for the state in the struggle for social justice
in any nation, and the needs to protect the disadvantaged nations in
'fair trade' and local jobs when markets are opened to foreign competition. This change of mind is an example of liberals sticking to their
basic principle: face the facts.

In morality and religion a liberal demands liberty for a discussion of
alternatives and, in that debate, supports positions which have taken
account of sound science or social reality. That is not to say that science
or society should dictate to morality or religion, for morality is concerned with what ought to be and religion with the reality without
which nothing can exist. It can be alleged that liberals do not care about
the difference between right and wrong, but that is not the case:
liberals ask what in the long run will be the consequences of a decision
for everyone involved in a situation which may not be simple. It can also
be said that liberals do not care about the truth in religion and merely
adopt fashionable ideas, but that also is not true, or at least ought never
to be true. Repeatedly Christian liberals have been ready to suffer
punishment because they have a thirst for truth and a conscience about
what they are expected to believe.

A 'liberal' interpretation of a text claimed to be authoritative means
being free to think about its context, seeing that every word belongs to
a sentence, every sentence to a passage, every passage to a larger statement with its own character and purpose. A myth is not a bit of science;
a poem is not a photograph; a story is not necessarily accurate history;
a law is not necessarily timeless. In ethics we may need new myths,
poems, stories and laws. And in religion this 'liberalism' of many mean-
ings can indicate the exercise of the freedom to think out, and decide for
oneself, when and how an authority, written or living, should be
obeyed. Recently conservative theologians have often announced that
'the Enlightenment is over', referring to the eighteenth-century prece-
dents for nineteenth-century liberalism. But the overthrow of outdated
authority meant mainly new inventions or ideas in technology and
politics making for the liberation of the people, and even when it
entered theology that liberation of thought seldom denied the reality of
God and often contrasted the reality of oppressive churches with the
example of Christ. Its greatest philosopher, Kant, summed it up. Dare to
ask, to find out, to know, to be wise! That challenge was startling but it
was emphatically not a command to stop thinking about religion and
morality.

A frequent criticism is that liberalism is shallow and narrow because
it is academic and rationalist. Blaise Pascal (a conservative Catholic)
famously pointed out long ago that the heart has its reasons, and in our
own century the heart does not need to be defended merely on the

ground that it too is reasonable. In an oral (mouth-to-mind) culture logic based on reading and writing can seem out of place, and one meaning when untraditional societies are called postmodern is that a culture is shaped by images, stories and songs more than by boring old men on platforms, and by TV and the internet more than by boring old books. But it does not follow that there is now no room for serious books and critically attentive readers, ultimately in the service not only of truth but also of people who have little time for reading and who apply their minds to practical matters, for most people do not want a religion to be untrue any more than they want technology to be unreliable. And even people who belong with all their hearts to the 'second modernity' – to the new age which, we can be told, dawned in the 1960s – do not like to be called slavish, uncultured, reactionary, intolerant, ignorant or unenlightened. The Enlightenment, a movement born in serious books by European writers, was a response to forms of church and society which seemed, and actually were, enemies of truth and life. It may now look outdated in a very different Europe, and even more so in other regions which have never been bookish, but when it spoke the truth and liberated life it made a contribution to human progress which should not be despised. In its time it began a new age.

It seems that without the conservation of much that is traditional there can be nothing in Christianity which deserves to be communicated – yet without deeply serious thought about how to communicate its essential substance the churches' message cannot mean much in a world very largely different from the world of the Bible and from the changing scenes in most of the history of the Church. So in this book the concentration will not be on the divisive labels 'conservative' and 'liberal'. It will be on facts and experiences which may unite; on what humanity is; on what Jesus was and is; and on what God is and will be. An attempt, which of course must be open to correction, will be made to find the truth about subjects which are difficult and delicate but which deserve attention because they are supremely important. If the truth can emerge from a completely honest study, one day it may be the basis of a religion neither 'conservative' nor 'liberal' in the terms of the present conflict but Christian, humane and full of the liberated life which as a matter of fact arose on the first Easter morning.

TWO

~

YES TO HUMANITY

W HAT WE NOW know about humanity is more wonderful than any myth that our remote ancestors were perfect. We are physical, although not made from mud. And being more than physical, we are miracles although modern science can explain a great deal about us. Either we are miracles in the non-religious sense of being freaks, something very, very strange produced by a universe which includes many accidents with no ultimate purpose – or else we are not strange at all in the final analysis, because we are developments intended from the beginning of all that exists. And science cannot make that decision for us, either way. What it can do is to give us fascinating facts.

Life on this planet began as a chemical process. This is now thought to have involved more than a thousand amino acids arranged in the right sequence which produced tiny strings of protein. Energised by the sun's rays, by Earth's hot interior and by its thick atmosphere, cells managed to stay together, to move and to reproduce themselves. This 'Big Birth' took place very roughly ten billion (thousand million) years after the birth of the universe in the 'Big Bang', but not much more than one billion years after the marriage of gas and dust which had resulted in the birth of planet Earth, orbiting around the sun in a pattern which would one day make life possible (and at a tilt which would one day make seasonal agriculture possible). Life, for long confined to bacteria, became structured as it used carbon, originally some of the scattering debris after the explosion of a giant star. Over hundreds of millions of years many multicellular organisms appeared and disappeared. Some used the land in order to breed a little more safely and the atmosphere became congenial as tiny organisms in the oceans, and a growing spread of plants in the richer soil, pumped out oxygen, but not too much of it. Five or six extinctions then eliminated most forms of life, but the growth of bones and limbs was surprisingly quick. Fish evolved into dinosaurs which reigned for more than 150 million years. They perished about 65 million years ago but were survived by rats. Rats became apes which found hands more useful than tails.

The decisive change, when apes became the first of many varieties of semi-human hominids in an African forest about five million years ago, was not willed or seen by any of them: there was an abnormality in the genes and this development was transmitted to a new generation when two apes enjoyed sex. When the forests diminished because the climate changed these hominids learned to walk on their feet; footprints about 3.6 million years old have been found. About two million years ago the intelligence of *Homo habilis* grew when using stones as tools. About one million years ago *Homo erectus* used stronger legs to walk out of Africa to Indonesia and North China. They also used fire and that meant that the meat needed by their bigger brain could be cooked and more easily digested. In its turn that meant that men needed to learn to co-operate in hunting while the women stayed near the domestic cave or other shelter, to take care of the children, to gather food from plants and to cook. It helped men and women to be mostly naked because they needed to sweat but they could cover themselves with other animals' skins when cold.

Some 400 thousand years ago another human species, of African origin but also found in the Middle East and Asia, had a still bigger brain. So Neanderthal Man could migrate, wrap up and survive in southern Europe for about 300 thousand years. But the most promising development was again in Africa: there most of the anatomy of *Homo sapiens* became 'modern' about 200 thousand years ago and brains evolved to their modern size about fifty thousand years later. Less than a hundred thousand years later a group which may have been quite small made its exodus from Africa across the bottom of the Red Sea, first staying near the beaches of the Indian Ocean where protein was easily available. Their multiplying successors reached Australia, moved up the Indus valley to Central Asia and China, crossed land at the top of the world to the Americas, and entered Europe where Neanderthal Man disappeared (because of them?). The brain had become smaller, probably because it was an advantage to reduce the pain of the skull's exit from the womb, but the genes could arrange for new brain cells and all the brain could be strengthened by the exercise of thinking so that enlargement after birth could be fourfold. Indeed, modern humans have called the sub-species which developed *Homo sapiens*, although the Latin is best translated as 'skilled' rather than 'wise'.

These ancestors of ours used fire to make metals about fifty thousand years ago, used artefacts as decoration about forty, painted pictures about thirty, made music about twenty, talked in a single but increasingly complex language about fifteen, farmed and built villages and religious shrines about ten, and began to write about five thousand

years ago. That, very roughly, is how long it really took to create Adam
and Eve, and over the whole process believers may recite Genesis 1:27:

> So God created humankind in his image,
> in the image of God he created them;
> male and female he created them.

And if we think that their bodies are the inferior parts of men and
women, we ought to meet the lovers in the scriptural Song of Songs.
Both are heavily scented. Both have black hair and hers is plaited with
ribbons. Both have bellies like ivory and that region of her offers a cup
filled with spiced wine. His head and arms look like gold and his legs are
like pillars of marble. Her neck is like a tower of ivory, her cheeks are
like fruit trees, her breasts are like clusters of grapes, her sandalled feet
are so beautiful that no comparison is possible. Her lips are like a
honeycomb and their kisses are intoxicating.

What is known scientifically about the human body in its current shape
also deserves celebration. It is very small and weak in comparison with
the dinosaurs and far more clumsy and slow than the birds, and most of
it consists of water, yet it is built with about 220 types of tissue in cells
beyond counting. It is the product of a genome first understood, at least
in outline, in research first published in 2001. Between sixty and eighty
thousand genes are combined by sexual intercourse to provide the
physical basis of a new personality, in a space smaller than the head of
a pin. When switched on by the passage of time, by external events or
by the brain itself, about half of these influence body-building, and
through that, behaviour. The rest have no known purpose but it is
known that changes in the pattern of the genes produce changes in the
sequence of amino acids in protein, with consequences which can be
great.

   Made possible by this genetic foundation, every perception, whether
a thought or a feeling or (as is usual) a very rapid combination of emotion and reasoning, is produced by one thing – the brain, a sludgy part
of the central nervous system which after its death may be extracted
from the skull and then does not look nearly so beautiful as the skin has
been on the skull's other side. It begins to grow two weeks after the
fertilisation of the egg and is recognisable two weeks later; it is almost
complete two years after birth but grows for another twenty years; it
begins to lose cells when thirty years old (perhaps the average time for
death during most of the history of *Homo*) and no cell can be replaced.
Its functioning can be changed drastically by disease, violence or sur-
gery as well as by old age, and when it dies the whole body dies. Its lifelong job is to process information fed to it by chemicals released by

nerves which have used electricity to speed their messages at about 250 miles an hour. This work is, we are told, done by about a hundred thousand million cells (neurons) connected chemically in many more junctions (synapses), and the result is achieved almost instantaneously and almost always with complete success.

The brain has two hemispheres, the left which (it seems) makes for right-handedness, for practical skills, for language and for logical analysis which includes critical questioning, and the right side which apparently makes for the more mysterious activities which are called intuition, creativity and spirituality. Ethical decisions seem to be taken in the front of the brain, also the home of thought and speech; this part was the last to be developed in evolution and is not fully developed in adolescents. The hypothalamus is the powerhouse of emotions; it is older and further back. In women the two hemispheres are slightly smaller but the *corpus callosum* which joins them is slightly larger, which seems to influence the ability of women to feel and do several things at the same time, to the wonderment of men. But we are warned that no one part of the brain seems to be exclusively responsible for any one activity and that no activity is isolated from all others. Although since 1990 brainscans have been so improved that neuroscientists have made spectacular advances in locating brainwork, the miracle of *Homo* remains a symphony and to a large extent a mystery.

It can be thought that modern knowledge of these facts has ruined our dignity because it has destroyed 'free will'. But the brain makes decisions every minute of our waking lives and none can be predicted with complete certainty unless they are reflexes (unconscious and involuntary reactions to stimuli). Decisions are made in response to pressures from our genes, the rest of our bodies, our environments or our memories, in a mixture where no one influence is so strong that we should speak of 'determinism' by a single force.

Decisions are made in the brain after consideration of memories formed out of previous experiences and stored at the back. These help us to watch and judge ourselves (so to speak), so that we become clever or good, but the bottom of each hemisphere is an amygdala, the source of strong emotions – especially fear – which can overwhelm the reasoning which goes on in the front. However triggered, the output of joy can even override the gene-based instincts of which the strongest is the will to survive. Thus a bungee jumper can throw a whole body into danger because the predominant desire is to experience the joy of a rush of chemicals from the adrenal gland. Or an adulterer may be pushed by an upsurge of hormones from the endocrine glands. Or a martyr, a soldier or a rescue worker may embrace, or at least risk, death because a voice within has been trained for years to speak of duty and honour whatever the cost. These are in a sense compulsions but on the whole, thanks to the plurality of influences in decision-making, *Homo sapiens* has more freedom than any other creature and the story of human evolution is a story of growing freedom.

It can also be thought that modern knowledge degrades personal relationships because it reduces us to the status of machines. But two of the most important strengths of the human brain are its abilities to understand and communicate with other humans, and to join them with a sensitive tact in a shared task. At point after point in the story of evolution these abilities were vital to progress. Often they have proved more effective in achieving success than any ability to impose one's will: one manages other people best by loving them and earning their love. And often these abilities have proved more important than the instincts to defend one's own territory ruthlessly and to seize an opportunity to control someone else's, for one's own group can prosper by doing a deal with the rivals.

Darwin made his decisive contribution to modernity by suggesting what has never been refuted: that evolution works by awarding prizes to those who are most successful, first in competing for limited resources, and then in breeding better-equipped successors. But effective competition has again and again involved effective co-operation, and skill or intuition in that department is not the least desirable part of the new generation's equipment. And after Darwin just as before him, it has been the human experience that life means knowing what a mother can give, then what family, friends and teachers can give, then what a partner can give, then what we can give to our offspring, then what a wider circle can give, so that we become fully ourselves through our relationships and find the meaning of our existence in what takes at least two people – love. And all that needs brainwork, which can include the still unexplained power of communication between brains called telepathy.

Another, and greater, danger to religion has come from the feeling that modern knowledge ends any hope that we can have reliable knowledge of the invisible and perpetually mysterious power called God in English. Darwin felt this acutely and we now know that more than 98 per cent of our genes are identical with those of the chimpanzee, from whose evolution our own diverged only some 300,000 generations ago. But so far as we know from research, only the human brain is able to think of any alternative to the instinctive behaviour dictated by the genes. Although other creatures perform many actions which we think clever or good, they do so because they have inherited instincts of which we approve. In contrast, *Homo sapiens* is able to ask what is reasonable or ethical in behaviour, being self-conscious and self-critical. And it seems that only the human brain has developed even further than that point. We can ask not only what was the immediate cause of an event but also what caused that cause – and we can ask what caused existence.

Religion in some shape appears to be a feature of life in every human society whose thoughts are to any extent understandable now. Recent explorations of the recesses of caves have shown that Ice Age Man painted pictures or made carvings of animals in places so difficult to reach that it seems that the intention was to please gods or spirits, not humans, and the pictures on view in places where there may have been gatherings may also have had a purpose other than decoration. That purpose may have been magic, but if so the ritual was other than the practical business of hunting and killing animals. It was an activity capable of developing into reasonable and moral religion.

It is known that care was taken in human burials some twenty-five thousand years ago, presumably in the belief that humans are special. Artefacts could also be buried, presumably in the hope that they would be of use when the dead live as spirits themselves, and most famously by the ancient Egyptians although they threw away brains. So far as we can know, humans are the only animals who long before death is imminent realise that one day they too are going to die, and who ask with deep emotion whether their deaths will be completely the end of their existence. This question is the mother of religion. What we know about long-dead societies is mostly based on what we possess of evidence that they struggled against the acceptance of total death as the universal fate. Even in a secularised modern society it usually seems right to mark a human death with some affirmation about human existence. Usually the local religious tradition is used because its words and music at least have the power to express an appropriate sense of mystery. *Homo sapiens* is, it seems, the animal that knows that death is inescapable, but hopes that it may be outlived, and so is the religious animal.

It does not follow that every individual has a developed religious sense, however, for especially in a modern society many people can lead good, enjoyable and useful lives in holes shielded from the mystery of the Whole. But a comparison can be made with the process by which the real world has an impact on the eyes which then needs to be transmitted to the brain through millions of fibres in the optic nerve. What then becomes 'sight' is an interpretation of our surroundings that may be defective if our genes have made us blind, short-sighted or colour-blind. In something of the same way, some people may be blind to the presence of God and even blind to the wonder that they exist. It seems to be useless to hope that they will 'see the light' and better to reflect that even forms of natural light may be invisible to the naked human eye.

If thinking is what the brain does, is it sensible to think about the possibility of life after the brain's death?

Certainly any such thinking must use images derived from the only world we know. The ultimate divine reality has to be pictured as a man or woman and eternity must be imagined as 'the other world' with other men, women and children in it, suitably clothed. Eternal glory has been seen as a royal court, or in a more democratic age as a holiday camp. But since what the brain does stops when the brain dies, what (if anything) is real after death can never be known for certain: it can only be imagined, perhaps in the light of what the brain imagines when near death. And the imagination should not run riot. The only logical alternative to the acceptance of death as the universal and irreversible fate of all that lives is, it seems, to believe that the personal identity which before death depended on the body's brain can after death depend on the ultimate reality called God. It must be somewhat like swimming in the ocean after walking on the beach – but the human situation on earth is that we have to walk while a fog hides the sea.

That eternal destination cannot be possible on the basis of our cleverness, goodness or correct believing, because all that is trivial in the context of eternity: we do not carry a child's plastic bucket into the ocean. It can be possible only if the ultimate reality is such that it can be joined by any creatures capable of such union, and so far as we know the only creatures so capable are human. That may seem intolerably arrogant of us but a clue that we are capable of eternity is provided by those peak moments in human experience when we are struck dumb in awe and bliss, and 'time stands still'. Perhaps we are moved by a view from a mountain, or by a newborn baby, or by music. Such ecstasies have been celebrated with famous eloquence, but they are also well known to the tongue-tied. They overwhelm us, but reveal to us what matters most about us and our environment. When such moments are reported it is often said that unusual light was experienced. Whether or not that was the case, they are moments of illumination and vision.

In the history of Christianity's relationship with modern science there have been phases. At first scientists thought of themselves as devout Christians investigating the facts about God's creation; then much more was known about the creation and it seemed incompatible with the Bible; then Bible believers produced theories about nature which turned out to be unsatisfactory either as science or as religion; and then much more was understood both about nature and about the Bible, and sound science could seem compatible with revised theology. At present, however, neither the public nor the churches seem to have taken much interest in this fourth phase. So a scientifically respectable Christian answer to the ancient question 'What is Man?' deserves to be learned and offered despite the obviously great risk of mistakes.

But there remains the question 'How, then, should humans behave?' and about that Christians are at present deeply divided, facing problems which may concern anyone intimately. If what is right is what is truly natural – for believers, a reflection of God's law for his creation – is it ever right to interfere in the natural process of dying? Is it ever right to remove from the womb what has been planted there by another natural process? Is it ever right to enjoy sex without intending what is often its natural result, the beginning of a new life? And is it ever right to accept sexual relationships which are not the natural mating of a man and a woman?

A scientific account of human nature does not use terms such as soul, spirit, conscience or will, and in its refusal to cut the unity of the human person into departments it happens to be quite close to the picture we see in the myths of the ancient Hebrews. For these, the Lord God turned 'dust' into 'a living being' when he 'breathed the breath of life' into it (Genesis 2:7). In contrast, some Greek philosophers (the greatest of them was Plato) can be quoted to the effect that the body is the prison of the soul. Partly because their revered teachers were taught that philosophy in former ages, many Christians have held that a soul or spirit (not merely God's breath) was added by God to Adam and Eve and that a new soul or spirit is given to every new human body at conception or not long after it. When a body dies this soul is taken back by God and what becomes of it then depends on whether the conscience, inspired by God, has guided the soul to have the right influence on the will and therefore on the heart and mind. If so, there will have been the right discipline over the desires of the flesh, which is always inclined to choose evil. Hopefully the soul will be given a new body in the general resurrection and will delight in the use of it in a new world, when the old flesh and earth have been glorified. Otherwise, the soul will be made physical enough to suffer endless anguish in hell. Many Christians have also believed that the soul can be purified by a limited time of lesser pain in purgatory, as penance for sins which made this a necessary preparation for heaven. But in each case the soul's use of a human body will have been important in the evidence used in the divine judgement.

That crude summary of traditional beliefs may be not too far from what many Christians still believe, and it may seem to be supported by how almost everyone feels. There does seem to be an 'I' behind the eyeballs which is more real than the 'me' whom I occasionally meet in the mirror. And it may influence how people who are not traditionally religious put things in everyday language. Whether or not we pray that God will have mercy on a soul, what is deeply emotional is called soulful and what is lively is called spirited, and we can praise someone's active conscience or determined willpower. The usual order of things in

New Age thinking does not begin with the mere body: it is 'mind, body . . .'

This traditional way of talking about ourselves has influenced the responses of churches and individual Christians to some important moral questions. It is in the background to the official teaching of the Roman Catholic Church, which is that human life is sacred from conception to natural death and that sexual intercourse is wrong if it is not open to the transmission of life during a period of natural fertility, or if it is not between a man and a woman who are married until death.

Many Christians have become unwilling to say simply that only God should be allowed to decide the question of life or death. Medicine is praised almost universally for its many interferences in natural illnesses. It is of course far less common to praise suicide, but in modern times there has been a large increase in sympathy with the mental distress which can end in such a tragedy, and this has been accompanied by a greater conviction that the rejection of God's gift of body-based life need not be followed by the impossibility of eternal life in the joys of God's mercy and of final fulfilment. There has also been a more publicly expressed growth of conviction that God is not being defied if a physician administers the divine gift of drugs in order to relieve very severe pain during the final stages of dying, with the side effect that this process ends mortal life more quickly. Far more questionable is the withdrawal of food and drink which have been given through a tube over a long period to a patient who is incurable and unconscious, but even this termination of a half-life, mercifully rare and requiring a judicial as well as an expertly medical decision, need not be thought utterly evil. Almost all Christians still condemn, as being obviously dangerous to the whole relationship between doctors and patients, the legalisation of deliberate suicide assisted by the physician while the patient is conscious and not near death – but in some such cases the agony which is still a fact on some deathbeds can make some authentically Christian consciences confused (as is widely thought) by compassion. It would seem that the discussion of such painfully difficult questions between Christians should not take the form of a battle. Here as elsewhere, the best question to ask is what is truly humane.

Total opposition to the artificial termination of an embryo at any stage, and to the use in potentially very beneficial medical research of stem cells stored as surplus in fertility clinics, is still influenced by the belief that an embryo has been given a 'soul' at conception. But difficulties in this belief are now widely recognised. Natural miscarriages are frequent and the division of embryos to form twins takes place after the one egg has been fertilised. To many Christians it now seems more realistic to think that 'soul' refers in this context to a human relationship with God, which begins after some development of the foetus at a time known only to God. That does not settle the argument about abortion or stem cells, because what is in the womb from conception is rapidly becoming a person to be honoured and loved with delight by God as well as by us – and therefore is already sacred in some sense. It is not surprising that when laws about abortion are being, or have been, changed in many countries Christians have been sharply divided in the discussion.

It seems essential to honour the convictions of those who do not think it right to have anything to do with any abortion, because from very early on Christianity has taught that this destruction of what is actually or potentially a human being is a sin. The legal position in (for example) Britain, that personality dates from the first breath outside the womb, does not take full account of recent knowledge of how well developed a foetus is at a stage earlier than was commonly thought. But the legalisation of some abortions by modern procedures in an early stage of pregnancy has been accepted or supported by many Christians as the lesser of two evils. In the canon law of the Roman Catholic Church before 1869 such abortions were not regarded as 'mortal' sins which would deserve hell if not repented, and in the Middle Ages Thomas Aquinas (following Aristotle) taught that a soul developed at about 40 days for a boy and 90 for a girl. In Britain the law rightly requires the approval of two doctors who know the situation, but at a very early stage this is not the killing of a child: it is a very sad sacrifice of potential life when the mother is in serious danger or would be very unlikely to love and care for the baby. It is to be hoped that the carefully moral thinking behind this position will be more widely accepted and that meanwhile neither side in the debate will claim that the other side is undeniably evil. What Christians must see as evil is 'abortion on demand' for a selfish reason, preventing the birth in order to pursue a career or maintain a lifestyle which has included sex without adequate precautions.

But another issue cannot be avoided if we are trying to be realistic. When it has been said that the flesh needs to be fought, most people, including most Christians, have thought about sex. So if we take modern knowledge and experience into account, what should Christians now decide about the ethics of human sexuality?

We now know that *Homo sapiens* is by nature not only a religious animal: this is also among the sexiest beings in nature, driven to be so by chemicals released by the brain. This animal has sex face to face and can be very willing to have it on most days or nights all the year round, with the possibility of orgasm as the biggest incentive for both genders.

These facts suggest that nature has no intention of giving this pleasure only to people who want a baby at this precise juncture – and this pleasure is, it seems, meant to be available to almost every adult who is not too old, for nature has not heard about formal marriage. However, the emotional intensity which does not seem to occur during and after the mating of any other animal, and the frequency of that emotion, suggest that nature has a special purpose here – to encourage the partners to stay together long enough to take care of a child who otherwise would be helpless for longer than the offspring of most animals.

We now know that nature is not interested in whether an individual starts life as male or female; indeed, in some cases the genes make the body one and the emotions the other. Everyone would be female had a male-making chromosome not caused another development in approximately a half of all conceptions. But it is crucially important that the heterosexual act should be possible and attractive because novelty and individuality depend on the combination of the male and female genes in the uterus. Nature seems willing to pay a heavy price for its use of this method of achieving progress and personality, for the genetic basis of a human body has to be so intricate that even nature can make a mistake. Usually a new life is so nearly a reproduction of its parents that the birth is successful, particularly so if the combination of the two sets of genes has transmitted some physical or mental feature which is an improvement in relation to the chances of survival and breeding in the given environment. But the result can be very serious disability, as in the birth of the child with an extra chromosome.

These realities date from when we first evolved, but sex has been experienced somewhat differently in the modern world. Better health has speeded up puberty; advertising has used sex to flavour almost anything it wants to sell; sexual suggestiveness is the easiest way to get an audience; parents and other elders have less control; more jobs are available and more financial needs are felt, so that contraception which prevents the arrival of an unwanted baby has been welcomed as offering pleasure which seems risk-free and guilt-free. In this new situation customs often practised in earlier times but not then thought to be completely respectable have ceased to be secret or shameful. Such customs include masturbation, sensual loving, love affairs consummated with consent, and cohabitation as a way of getting to know thoroughly a person whom one might marry but who at present shares one's own reluctance to turn this intimate relationship into a legal marriage which runs the risk of a legal divorce, often involving great distress. An understanding of 'chastity' which simply condemns all such practices is not now accepted even as an ideal by most people in modern societies.

Many Christians continue to believe deeply that such practices are wrong and many (in our time as in earlier periods) have accepted the need for self-control or self-sacrifice with great difficulty but unseen heroism. All Christians should respect that integrity, should use it as a challenge to think again, and should share conservative attitudes at least to the extent that promiscuity or other forms of loveless sex are strongly rejected. But it may also be accepted by all Christians, if only as a matter of fact, that traditional teaching was related to traditional societies. In them almost everyone married. Women were usually married, or engaged to be married, hopefully as virgins and usually not long after puberty, by arrangements in which both families played decisive or large roles. Since many children died in their early years, it was hoped that many would be born. A woman was likely to die within twenty years of her marriage, her primary or only role apart from breeding having been to support her husband and children by hard work in the home or the field. A man was often expected to have some sexual experience before marriage but society condemned him if he deflowered a virgin without marrying her. It did not approve of adultery but usually blamed the woman as 'Eve the Temptress', and allowed the man to divorce his wife. Customs varied as to what defects would have to be alleged, what property she should retain, and whether she could initiate the divorce, but the law of ancient Israel allowed a husband to choose it merely if he found 'something objectionable in her' (Deuteronomy 24:1–3). Often she would have to earn her living by selling the use of her one acknowledged asset to anyone interested. Divorced wives must have been numerous among the prostitutes whose friend Jesus was.

Modern customs have another ideal. Teenage pregnancies are disasters, not blessings, and during one's first twenty-five years it is usually regarded as best to be without children. All earlier relationships may be regarded as preparation for a satisfying marriage based on romantic love and deep friendship. This will be regarded as a partnership between equals who could survive if separated, and if it is ended, any property will be divided by a court, often in equal shares. Hopefully it will result in a desired but limited number of children and will be creatively happy for forty years or more, but provision must be made for the ending of a relationship which, very sadly, has become very unhappy and very destructive precisely because its emotional basis has changed. At different paces Christians and their churches have been moving towards an acceptance of these modern marriage customs, believing that what Jesus taught about the Sabbath, saying that it was 'made for humankind' (Mark 2:27), applies also to marriage. This is an institution blessed by God because it comes as near as possible to

making two people 'one flesh' until death, and the nearer anyone comes
to that joy, the better, but marriage was not made to be a chain.
Obviously modern marriage has its problems, but these can be
regarded as the price paid for its advantages, particularly for women,
and the problems may well be reduced as it is increasingly seen that
there are advantages in the Christian position that, while marriage is
'natural' and not a Christian discovery, it is best to begin it with solemn
vows 'before God' to make the commitment unconditional and lifelong.

Jesus said that to divorce a wife according to the customs of his time
was as bad as adultery (Mark 10:2–11) – and adultery was very bad: if
an eye or hand tempts, it is better to destroy that (Matthew 5:17–19).
But such teaching was evidently not intended as precise legislation and
soon Christian teachers were permitting divorce for adultery (Matthew
5:32) or a second marriage after desertion by an unbelieving partner
(which seems to be the meaning of 1 Corinthians 7:12–16). Modern
Christianity has gradually simplified such exceptions made on pastoral
grounds into a general rule: the irretrievable breakdown of a marriage
in the eyes of both partners need not prevent a second marriage with a
more mature commitment to the responsibilities involved. But it does
not necessarily follow that the second wedding should take place in a
church or with the full ceremony, for the members of that church are
entitled to decide whether that is appropriate in the circumstances.
What seems wrong to most Christians in a modern society is that such
a marriage should lead to excommunication by a church. Providing
every encouragement to help the second marriage to work, and to last
in great happiness and creativity, is seen as the more truly Christian
attitude because more Christlike and more creative.

In brief, those who teach churches would be wise to acknowledge
more fully what nature teaches about heterosexual instincts and what
modern experience teaches about marriage between free equals. Then
they would be more realistic about facts.

A similar answer can be given to the question whether a homosexual
partnership can be 'blessed'. This question is acute in a society where
public opinion has so changed in recent years that such partnerships
can be registered for some important practical purposes by a democratic state. Whether a blessing should be given in public is again for a
church to decide but what matters far more is the possibility of a blessing by God, an act out of our control. For that a prayer would not be a
sin. In ancient Israel homosexual acts were regarded as an abomination
which deserved death or exile (Leviticus 18:22, 29) and Paul, believing
that they were a scandalous perversity, thought them a sin which
excluded the guilty from the kingdom of God (Romans 1:26–32; 1
Corinthians 6:9–10). But a homosexual orientation is now known to be

caused not by a choice to be evil but by a combination of genetic influence with early experience. So it is 'natural' for some men and women, as it is for some other animals, despite its obvious disadvantage in the breeding which powers evolution. It is also recognised that in many generations homosexuals have made major contributions to the evolution of the arts and society, church life and the kingdom of God. These are great steps forward into knowing the truth. But here as in all sexual relationships self-control and discretion are virtues for Christians as for everyone else. If self-fulfilment through practices which many people still do not think are 'natural' is given publicity as if it presented no problem at all, hostility is often provoked. So sensitivity is needed when, for example, it is claimed that homosexuals in actively sexual relationships have equal rights to be church leaders. Practising Christians will remember Paul's rebuke to those who 'knew' that eating food known to have been sacrificed in temples should not offend: some Christians would be offended and 'by your knowledge those weak believers for whom Christ died are destroyed' (1 Corinthians 8:11). Properly speaking, no one has a right to lead a church: it is for the church to call, on its own terms. While churches do well to remember how many of the best leaders in the past, including the recent past, were homosexuals (not necessarily 'practising'), homosexuals should not forget that an offer to lead because of a felt vocation may result in an invitation to suffer as Christ himself did (Mark 10:35–40).

From these questions I turn with relief to the man in whom Christians find God. A remarkable story printed nowadays in the fourth gospel (8:1–11) does not sound strict enough to be Johannine and may well have been added to some manuscripts from another source, but it relates that Jesus stopped the killing of a woman caught in adultery by inviting a man without a sexual sin to throw the first stone. If we work through evidence about Jesus we shall often have cause to ask whether in current controversies either conservatives or liberals are entitled to throw stones at other people who by being too strict or too lax have made mistakes in handling one of God's best gifts, sexuality. We meet a Jesus who combines the highest of ideals with the largest compassion, because he knows what it can and does mean to be human. We meet a judge whose combination of these normally incompatible attitudes is a large part of his timeless power to attract and to command. And thus we can meet the God whose tough love is here made human flesh, presumably knowing sexuality from the inside. When confronting a moral problem, the thoughtful Christian has to consider what is natural, what is humane, what Scripture says, what one's church teaches and what one's society respects – but also, and supremely, the shock that comes when Jesus steps out of the gospels.

THREE

❧

YES TO HIM THEN

'But who do you say that I am?' According to Mark (8:27) Jesus asked that question of his disciples shortly before he died. It does not sound as if he had previously explained at any length who he thought he was. He had lived his life, had told stories, and had uttered sharp sayings, without a pause for anything more systematic. It was a strategy which left every generation and individual with work to do: it seems presumptuous to answer his question, but he asks it. So I offer a summary of what seems true or highly probable about the historical Jesus and of what seems to have been really experienced about the eternal Christ. Plenty of room is left for other interpretations of the evidence, more traditional or radical, and of course many such interpretations are now available, but this sketch is based on the work of competent scholars over two hundred years and I have not tried to be sensational, for the facts are interesting enough.

The New Testament does not include a biography of Jesus in the modern style: there is no study of his personality as this developed in the course of accurately recorded events. He is never quoted directly. None of the evidence is in the Aramaic language which he used and the earliest known writing about him, the letters of Paul, provides very few detailed references to his life or teaching, although presumably Paul often spoke about such things in order to explain who was this 'Christ'. The oldest gospel in the New Testament, Mark's, is thought to have been written about thirty-five or forty years after the crucifixion. Many years later it was recorded that Papias, who had been born at about the same date, had said that it had been written shortly after the martyrdom of Peter by Mark who had been his assistant and 'interpreter', and as we shall see its content is compatible with this origin: it has been called a 'gospel for martyrs'. It is brief and urgent, and it does not say much about what Jesus taught.

Between AD 80 and 95 the gospels traditionally attributed to Matthew and Luke were offered as replacements. They probably used a document now called Q, which collected reports of the sayings (and one miracle) of Jesus. Presumably it had originated in the memories of people who had heard Jesus teach, but even if Papias can be relied on when he records the tradition that the apostle Matthew collected 'oracles in Hebrew', half a century had passed between the death of Jesus and the use made of this document in the new gospels in Greek. There cannot have been detailed accuracy in the transmission of the original words.

'Matthew' derived about half his gospel from Q and reproduced about 90 per cent of Mark's, adding his own material which forms about a quarter of the total work. This writer is preoccupied by the tension between the acceptance and the rejection of the Jewish religious law, including sayings which point in different directions. Possibly he hints at his own ambition as a Jewish Christian writer when he gives us a glimpse of the trained scribe who treasures both the old and the new (14:51–53). But he is unlikely to be the Matthew who had collected taxes.

'Luke', whose identity is to be discussed later, reproduced less of 'Mark' and about a third of his gospel was his own, with a discernible editorial slant: he stresses the Spirit, the parables and the appeal to women, outcasts and foreigners. Probably himself a Gentile, he writes good Greek and dedicates his book to Theophilus ('Lover of God'), claiming that it is 'orderly' and based on investigations. These were into events which had occurred approximately in the order outlined by 'Mark', but he was not an eyewitness and his chief inspiration is to tell tales vividly, retelling the parables of Jesus and adding his own stories-with-a-purpose in his second volume, the Acts of the Apostles. Thus he begins his gospel with a story about a conversation between an angel and an old priest more than eighty years previously. Theophilus would not have been put off, for in the ancient world no historian known to us confined himself strictly to facts.

That summary of a massive investigation by modern scholars may be enough to show the contrast with the Qur'an, whose contents were assembled not long after the Prophet's death in order to rule all Muslim faith. Many facts not included in these gospels have not been recovered, and never will be; for example, no copy of the sayings source has been found. And it is certain both that all the material now available had a history before it was incorporated into the Bible, and that there was a human element in that history. As it travelled from mouth to mouth it was liable to be changed or enlarged, and both 'Matthew' and 'Luke' felt free to use both 'Mark' and Q in slightly different ways, either because they used different versions or because they adapted the material to fit their own themes. And above all, these three gospels were, like their sources, shaped by Christian faith. This is even more characteristic of the fourth gospel, probably written about AD 95. As we shall see, a

deeply spiritual meditation by 'John' does not owe much to memory or
to research.

A few brief references in Jewish or Roman sources are more detached,
but when in a rabbinic source Jesus was a 'magician' who deserved to be
'hanged', or when Josephus calls him 'a wise man' who did 'startling
deeds', or when the contemptuous Tacitus confirms that he was executed under Pontius Pilate, or when Suetonius thinks that 'Chrestus'
had caused rioting in Rome, we do not learn much. Some other sayings
scattered in gospels not admitted to the Church's Bible may be authentic words of Jesus but on the whole those gospels are incompatible with
the main evidence, which is older. One problem about a tendency in
them – and in some modern reconstructions – is that it is hard to see
why a teacher of personal spirituality who was both other-worldly and
enigmatic was considered to be such a danger to the authorities that he
had to be executed. What is shown is that fascination with Jesus already
took a variety of forms in the first two Christian centuries. It has of
course never ended and never lost its diversity.

If we are looking for reliable evidence about the true history of Jesus
of Nazareth, it seems sensible to start by asking whether any of the surviving material originated in a time when people could remember seeing and hearing him. And it seems helpful to look first in the obvious
places – the Lord's Prayer, which the early Christians used as a model
for their own praying because they believed that their Lord had taught
it; the parables which, although retold in the gospels, reflect rural life in
Galilee as an urgent message is communicated to country folk; the
moral teaching now gathered in the Sermon on the Mount which does
not legislate about day-to-day problems but is memorable because very
unconventional; and the reports of miracles in Mark's gospel, illustrat-
ing the activities of a healer using methods usual at that time but with
an unusual message.

If we feel that there can be nothing fresh in it now, in the Lord's Prayer
we should notice the silences. Christians are not told to empty their
minds, as is recommended in some forms of meditation; we are told to
fill our minds with thoughts about God. But we do not need to adore
him, or even to thank him, with many words. We also need not pray for
spiritual enlightenment through a full understanding of God's nature,
plans and methods. Nor is there prayer for Israel, or for the Church.
There is not even prayer for admission to heaven: instead we are told to
think about God as a 'father' and 'king' who may rule us in this mortal
life and all this world. Instead of asking for strength to do great deeds,
or for the privilege of seeing great marvels, we are told to pray for a day's
food, for much-needed forgiveness, and to be spared tests which we

should be bound to fail. There is no prayer about any other problem or adversity. Nor is there any prayer about Jesus himself, because to say Yes to him is to say Yes to his vision of God and his 'kingdom' or royal rule. But of course we are left free to pray about anything.

There are two versions of the Lord's Prayer – an indication that the early Christians did not feel obliged to reproduce the exact words of Jesus. Luke 11:2–4, being the shorter, is likely to be the older. It begins by calling God not by any often used title such as 'king of the universe' but as 'Father'. In Aramaic *abba* expressed a child's dependence (it could be at a baby's first word, like *dadda*) but also an adult's affectionate respect. Although the comparison of God with a father who acts like a mother is often found elsewhere, this degree of intimacy is not quite matched in any religion not dependent on Jesus. Paul recorded that the Christians in Galatia prayed to 'Abba! Father!' (4:6), as did the Christians in Rome (8:15). In this single, elementary word is summed up the faith that the force behind the universe created humans in an act of love. And the other version, Matthew 6:9–13, adds 'our' to *Abba*, showing that this prayer is not only for the individual. It is also for the new family drawn together around Jesus and potentially is for everyone.

Calling the Creator of all that exists or is possible 'Daddy' could make us casual or sentimental, so Matthew's version adds a warning. Abba is neither male nor female, both close and mysterious, both disclosed and distant, because 'in the heavens' – although presumably the reference to the sky does not imply any denial that he is also all around us on this planet and deep within us. In the gospels when Jesus prays to be spared crucifixion, 'distressed and agitated' (Mark 14:33), 'with sweat like great drops of blood' (Luke 22:44), his petition is to Abba and it is not granted. His followers do well to approach Abba with similar awe.

Both versions teach that the Creator's 'name' is to be 'hallowed'. The primary meaning is prayer that he may show what he is – great beyond the best we can see or imagine (he is no idol), and holy, holy, holy beyond all human praise (which he does not need). At a time when the distinction between God and Jesus was no longer complete, Mark reported a protest by Jesus himself: 'Why do you call me good? No one is good but God alone' (10:18).

To say Yes to this son and spokesman of God is also to say Yes to his cause, the kingdom of God on earth. We are not told to pray for a more prosperous world, or for inspiration to build such a future, and we are not to ask for excellence in our own spiritual or moral progress while the world remains unsatisfactory. Instead we are told to pray that God's government may be acknowledged as fully 'on earth' as it is in eternity – and there is no further specification. This petition implies that the most we can offer is co-operation at a very junior level, for this kingdom 'comes' by ways and stages to be decided by its king. But Matthew adds a description which is adequate: God's kingdom 'comes' when God's will is done.

If we are to live and work in the full-time service of that cause, we need food and our creative Father will provide it – but not necessarily in abundance. We are to pray for enough food for one day, the day ahead as we pray in the morning or evening. And where necessary this food will be made palatable and digestible by the skills which God has given, turning wheat into bread. Jesus of Nazareth, countryman and carpenter, knew from inside both nature and the world of work. Of course he accepted that humans do not 'live by bread alone', but he also accepted that to be human is to be physical before one can be spiritual: one must have breakfast before a day's work for the kingdom.

Although superbly well equipped to tend, enjoy and use God's good creation, we have often decided to vandalise it and to damage or destroy others or ourselves. We must, and can, rely on his forgiveness – but on one condition: we must be ready to forgive any who have wrecked or damaged us. Luke's version refers to 'sins' but Matthew's has 'debts'. Originally the Lord's Prayer was for use by poor people who were often in debt, so that the burden of sin is compared with the burden of debt, and forgiveness-all-round with the delight of a great debt's total cancellation, and any sin against God or neighbour is like a failure to pay what we owe to our Maker or to others. Here a feature of life and God's government is implied clearly enough: we must be cleansed from the poisons of hatred and contempt. The anger of Jesus was reserved for people too proud to think that they did not need to take and give forgiveness. This is expressed in the story of the slave who is forgiven an immense debt by his master and then demands a far smaller sum from a fellow slave (Matthew 18:23–35).

The final petition in Luke's version asks to be spared the 'time of trial'. This refers not to minor temptations but to a fearful conflict between good and evil when obedience to God is likely to bring suffering to Jesus and to many of the best Christians. Here is a hope that, since most of us lack the spiritual strength to wear a martyr's crown, we may not be summoned into a crisis which would probably leave us uncrowned and in the dirt. Jesus was a revolutionary who in the end accepted his own death but whose followers were allowed to escape at that time: they were not yet ready to be tested by the power of evil. He did not underestimate the 'time of trial' predicted in Scripture, which might be 'a time of anguish such as has never occurred since nations first came into existence' (Daniel 12:1).

Matthew's version adds a prayer for rescue 'from the Evil One', probably added when beliefs that the 'time of trial' would reach its climax in the brutal Roman reconquest of Palestine (AD 66–74) had been replaced by the realisation that history would continue and remain under the power of Satan. (This is the Hebrew name for the Adversary, personifying all that it is at any time contrary to the will of God.) Some manuscripts of Matthew also add 'for the kingdom and the power and the glory are yours forever. Amen.' This epilogue had become the custom in churches which felt the need to reaffirm that although his 'kingdom' has not 'come' on earth as expected, God is already enthroned in eternity.

To say Yes to Jesus is also to think about the stories he told. They are retold in the gospels (with a special skill by Luke) but their background is still the life he knew in Galilee – which argues for their authenticity. Early Christian teachers such as Paul and John came from very different backgrounds and used styles very different from his. Jewish rabbis, in approximately his time or later, did tell homely stories to illustrate their interpretations of Scripture or the supplementary laws, but the parables of Jesus are far more numerous, far more substantial and far more provocative.

They are a reminder, however, that he was a Jew. He did not teach about unchanging realities in the style of some Greek philosophers. He did not organise his thoughts – or other people – with the cold logic for which Latin was the best language. Least of all was he willing to impose his teaching on other people by force. After a lot of prayer he thought and taught by using his intuition as he penetrated into the deepest meaning of his heritage as a Jew, and then by making up new stories set in familiar situations but suggesting unfamiliar interpretations. Often these stories would claim that the goodness to be seen in ordinary men and women makes them dear to God – indeed, makes them like God and able to be united with God. This is not a theme which many religious teachers have developed. And listeners were left to decide what a story meant to them – another unusual practice in preaching. To many it meant little: they heard but did not understand, so that Mark (4:10–18) could think that the parables were told in order to be puzzling. But Matthew (13:10–17) saw that this was itself a misunderstanding, and the intensive recent discussion by scholars has agreed that the parables were effective weapons. And although we cannot be sure that we are reading the actual words spoken by Jesus, it is reassuring to reflect that stories can be remembered more accurately than more theoretical statements, and that the themes in this teaching can be seen behind more than one story.

Several stories are about a feast, for this message about the Father's goodness is the best possible news. Friends invited to a dinner may plead other engagements but the poor, the disabled and the blind are welcomed and other people are dragged in, by order of the persistent host (Luke 14:15–24). The feast is prepared for the stupid son who has made a mess of his independence: when he returns home in shame his father runs towards him to be his host, and when the stay-at-home son sulks the father tells him to greet 'your brother' and urges him to eat, drink and be merry (Luke 15:11–32). Although it has often been said that Jesus wants our lives to be hard journeys or tough battles, it seems that he preferred the image of an urgent summons to a banquet.

He did not minimise the urgency. He compared a sensible reaction to his good news about God with the discovery of treasure known to be in a field for sale, or of a very valuable pearl known to be hidden in cheap junk (Matthew 13:44, 45). It may be carried by unworthy messengers, but the message is news about One who is compared with a shepherd tireless in search for one lost sheep, or a woman who sweeps a dark cottage in order to find one lost coin (Luke 13:44, 45). Distinguishing himself from a hellfire preacher such as John the Baptist, Jesus compares his disciples with children playing at weddings, not funerals (Luke 7:31).

But he wants his hearers to see that the invitation is urgent. He surprises by telling them to act like a guilty man who has a chance to buy off his accuser while they are both on their way to court, or like a dishonest employee who has a chance to provide for his compulsory retirement, or like a smart investor (Luke 12:57–59, 16:1–9, 19:11–27). They must not resemble the rich fool who thinks he has all the time in the world, not knowing that his comfortable life is about to be ended by death (Luke 12:13–21).

They must take thought about the right preparation for a banquet, not like the man who could not be bothered to put on a clean robe (Matthew 22:11–14). And they must be prepared to wait for the wedding, not like the bridesmaids who did not bring enough oil to replenish their little lamps in case there was a delay that evening (Matthew 25:1–13). Many of the parables are about a possible delay bringing disappointment. As they are retold in the gospels no doubt the concentration is on the delay in the promised return of the Lord in triumph, but originally the message was probably that just as the 'coming' of the kingdom of God had been delayed in the past, so it might be in the present or the future. Slaves must behave in their master's absence (Luke 12:35–40; Matthew 24:45–51). Building a tower or waging a war may take longer and cost more than expected (Luke 14:23–33). A crop will include weeds and not every fish caught will be saleable (Mark 4:1–19; Matthew 13:24–31, 47–48). A fig tree must be cared for (Luke 13:6, 21:29–31), a mustard tree must be allowed to grow from a tiny seed (Mark 4:30–32), yeast will not immediately leaven flour (Luke 13:20).

God is a model of patience, like the owner of a vineyard who does not take immediate action when his agents are beaten up by his tenants (Mark 12:1–12). We may grumble about God's inaction or unfairness but our proper response is to be grateful for what we have. Labourers who would otherwise be unemployed should be thankful that all are paid for a day's work at the standard rate, whatever the time worked (Matthew 20:1–15). Those who complain that God allowed Pilate to kill Jews in the temple, or a collapsing tower to kill eighteen people, should give thanks that although sinners they are still alive because of this divine patience (Luke 13:1–5).

When a flood comes, a house will stand only if it has strong foundations (Matthew 7:24–27), and when the flood has gone and the house has been cleaned, it should not be left empty or devils will make themselves at home (Luke 6:47–49, 11:24–26). People should keep praying fervently, as when a widow badgers a judge for justice (Luke 18:1–8), or a neighbour wakes up a family which may have bread to lend in an emergency, or when a hungry child asks for an egg and does not expect to be given a scorpion (Luke 11:5–12).

It is equally essential to be always sincere and genuinely humble, not like the son who promises to go to work and does not (Matthew 21:28–32), or like the Pharisee who boasts while praying (Luke 18:9–14). Such people are blind to realities and one blind man cannot guide another, any more than a man with a plank in his eye can see to remove a spot of grit in someone else's eye (Luke 6:39–42). The guest who is honoured most is one who takes a humble place and the host who is honoured most is the one who is hospitable to the poor (Luke 14:7–14). The man in the street who is praised is not one of those associated with the temple and anxious to preserve their ritual purity: he is the Samaritan willing to be seen to associate with a Jew who has been mugged (Luke 10:29–37). The one who is given eternal life is not the one who has said 'Lord, Lord' to Jesus. It is the one who has cared for the hungry, the thirsty, the stranger and the prisoner (Matthew 7:21, 25:31–46).

To say Yes to the message of Jesus is also to be challenged by how he lived. He was a scandal to many because he had suppers with tax collectors who collaborated with a hated government and with 'sinners' such as prostitutes, all believed to be unclean. Moreover, he enjoyed these meals although he knew that he was called a glutton and a drunkard (Luke 7:34). So far as we know he was never accused of any worse sin, yet in his purity he was unlike the monks who had retreated

into the desert around the Dead Sea or the Pharisees who kept themselves as meticulously free from pollution as the priests in the Jerusalem
temple were supposed to be.

He was a missionary and his mission made him abandon respect-
ability. While foxes have holes and birds have the nests, this skilled carpenter chose to be homeless (Luke 9:58) and depended financially on
women who followed him closely – too closely, as some no doubt
observed (Luke 8:1–3, 23:49). The urgency of this mission could not
allow would-be followers to ask for a father's permission or to wait for
a father's death (Luke 9:59–62). His messengers were told to carry no
staff for self-defence, no bag for food and no money (Luke 9:3). They
were to go barefoot and with no second tunic (Matthew 10:10). In no
way should they be superior to the poorest or the most despised, or
decline any food offered when given a night's shelter. They should imi-
tate not the gentry but the children, for they must behave as 'the
children of the Most High' (Luke 6:35). 'Unless you change and become
like children you will never enter the kingdom of heaven' – that must be
their message. And if you make a child stumble, 'it would be better for
you if a great millstone were fastened around your neck and you were
drowned in the depth of the sea' – that must be their warning (Matthew
18:1–6).

The main points in what he taught about ethics, by life and words
without any conventional preaching, are assembled by Matthew (5:1—
7:29). Again he asks his hearers to use their brains, for he makes his
words memorable by avoiding platitudes; he exaggerates and leaves the
down-to-earth implications to others; he is witty; he likes epigrams. He
teaches both awe and love for the Father, saying that power from God is
promised to the destitute who hunger and thirst for 'righteousness',
meaning both justice and goodness. These lucky people are the sorrow-
ful, the merciful, the peacemakers, the persecuted and the reviled.
Because God, and God alone, is trustworthy, there must be a calm
reliance on him – no anger or lust, no anxiety or arrogance, for those
sins arise from a wrong way of being dependent on others. A quiet
sincerity must replace publicity for piety or chastity. Not only is God
never to be named lightly: he is not even to be invoked while taking an
oath. Accordingly Matthew prefers 'the kingdom of heaven' to 'of God'
throughout his gospel. Nowhere in this teaching is there a law stating
which offences deserve which punishments; a warning that if one calls
someone a fool one becomes liable to hell is not a law. Nor is there a
judicious compromise; 'be perfect as your heavenly Father is perfect' is
not that. Least of all is this teaching a manual giving shrewd instructions about the problems of politics. Those who heard it were politically powerless.

The miracles of Jesus in the gospel of Mark are tougher on the modern-minded. Instead of events occurring naturally as they do in the parables, and spiritual strength being provided to the distressed as it is in the Sermon on the Mount, here natural 'laws' are broken, and diseases and disabilities ended, by supernatural interventions which can look like magic. Healings can occur without personal contact; a squall on a lake is stilled by a command and the water is walked on; a large crowd is fed by loaves which have not been baked and fish which have not been caught; the daughter of Jairus is brought back from death; a fig tree is cursed and withered because it has not produced fruit out of season; and often diseases caused by demons are cured by exorcism. We are told in the gospels that even in an age which we should regard as credulous such miracles did not convince everyone (e.g. Luke 10:13–16), and in our own time merely repeating these stories does not convince people with doubts about whether God acts in any way at all. Intellectual difficulties have to be faced now, as cries for help were answered some two thousand years ago in a culture which was not modern.

Many stories about marvels may be found in the history of religion, mysticism and (recently) parapsychology, but unless the evidence is exceptionally strong, and preferably supported by witnesses not inclined to believe, the natural modern reaction is scepticism. And certainly Jesus did not wish to be judged as a kind of magician, for he did not regard miracle-working as his chief task. He said it was 'evil' to ask for proof of his claims by a 'sign' and responded to such requests with a deep sigh or an exclamation about a 'wicked, godless generation' (Mark 8:11; Matthew 12:39). 'How much longer must I put up with you?' (Mark 9:19). He refused to set up a clinic in Capernaum (Mark 1:21–39) because he had to be on the road with his message. What separated him from magic was that he concentrated on the power of God instead of using spells to make things happen.

Some stories may have originated in post-Easter experiences: did disciples who had resumed their jobs as fishermen, but with troubled minds, see Jesus walking on the troubled water? And some may have grown out of earlier events, such as the history which may be discerned beneath Mark's two strangely different stories of the feeding of thousands (6:30–44, 14:13–21): Jesus may have calmed an overexcited crowd by making them sit down to eat their picnics when according to John's gospel they were planning to take him by force and make him king (6:15). Mark's story about a fig tree may have developed out of a parable (11:12–14, 20–24) and the daughter of Jairus, although believed to be dead, may have been sleeping in a coma as was suggested at the time (5:39).

However, many of the healings can be understood as real in modern terms. Some people have extraordinary abilities to influence others and we seem to be only at the beginning of an understanding of how the mind can influence one's own body or other minds or perhaps bodies. All the evidence shows that Jesus was charismatic because on fire with conviction about God and his own mission. The power of God communicated by this agent could, it seems, reach and affect the working of another's brain and could prove stronger than the power of the demons who had, it was believed, created the disorder by invading the body. It was said that 'he commands even the unclean spirits' (Mark 1:27). This belief, enabling Jesus to inspire a victim's brain to end a body's disorder, had (it seems) to be shared by Jesus and victim: if it was, it could heal.

Two of the thirteen miracles in Mark's gospel are cures of epilepsy which is caused by an electric storm in the brain. Others are cures of paralysis in legs, arm or hand, or of defective hearing or eyesight, or of skin diseases (not leprosy). We are not told whether or not the illness was complete or the cure permanent. One cure is of a woman who has suffered for many years from haemorrhages. Although she is unclean she boldly touches his tunic, Jesus feels power leaving him, and she is healed with the assurance that 'your faith has made you well' (5:25–34). A man is told that 'your sins are forgiven' because it was believed that someone could be paralysed by guilt and Jesus, although human ('the Son of Man') and a layman, takes his repentance for granted and assures him of God's forgiveness with no need to wait for the prescribed purification by ritual washing and sacrifice in the temple (2:1–12). In all these cases physiology is linked with psychology, which would amaze no modern doctor.

In Luke's gospel (7:18–23) Jesus explains why he cured anyone. When the imprisoned and disappointed John the Baptist sent messengers to ask whether he really was 'the one who is to come', Jesus advised him to think again about what he was doing in connection with biblical promises, for he had come not to denounce but to liberate. And when accused of working in league with the Evil One, he pointed out that although he was not the only miracle-worker in Galilee, his own motive went beyond healing an individual. He worked in order that some might understand that by this exercise of the 'finger' or power of God 'the kingdom of God has come upon you' (11:14–23). In contrast, his contemporaries who were monks in Qumran near the Dead Sea excluded from their community the very categories to whom Jesus went: the blind, the lame, the deaf and the dumb. He was a physician sent to the sick (Mark 2:17).

From the first the gospel could sound political. Mark (1:15) sums up the message which Jesus proclaimed: 'The time is fulfilled and the kingdom of God has come near; repent, and believe the good news.' But that was not how his message was expressed by the two great men who were to try to communicate it to seekers of spiritual truth. 'Kingdom of God' is used little in Paul's surviving letters, and there it means a future which can be inherited by being deserved and entered; it is a reward for Christian faith and life. In John's gospel (3:3–12) it means 'heavenly things'.

For Jesus, to speak about God's kingdom is to say that his government of the world is beginning, but because the emphasis could be either on the present or on the future there is some ambiguity in Mark's little collection of sayings about this kingdom. His introductory summary (1:14) may be understood in two ways: either the kingdom has arrived and so is 'near you', or it is near in time. Later we are told that Jesus never spoke in public about the kingdom except in parables, although he could explain them in private (4:2, 10). The secret may be revealed when Jesus is reported as saying 'there are some standing here who will not taste death until they see that the kingdom of God has come with power' (9:1), but reflection reveals ambiguity here also. The reference may be to the end of history when Jesus will come 'in the glory of the Father and the holy angels' (8:38), or it may be to the time when Jesus will 'go through many sufferings' but be raised from the dead (9:2–13). But it is also possible that in a time of many excitements – Peter and Paul martyred, the church in Rome full of fear, the Roman empire at war with Israel – Mark has incorporated a promise by a Christian prophet.

In Matthew's gospel (10:23) disciples are told that they will not have completed a mission to 'the towns' of Israel 'before the Son of Man comes'. This expression 'Son of Man' sounds odd in Greek (as in English) and is almost never found in Jewish literature. But it occurs 82 times in the gospels and it seems that usually Jesus was referring to himself modestly, as 'a man such as me' (our 'one'). However, in this passage as in some others there is almost certainly a reference to a grand vision of a symbolic figure who is 'like a man' and who goes in the clouds to the Ancient One to be vindicated and given 'dominion and glory and kingship, that all peoples, nations and languages should serve him' (Daniel 7:13–14). Originally this figure had personified Israel's hopes but 'Son of Man' could be used out of that context and Jesus may well have used it because of this double meaning of present humility and coming exaltation.

When Matthew reported that Jesus had believed that he would soon be vindicated, this gospel-writer himself believed that his Lord had been right: he had been raised from the dead so that now he could command his followers to 'go and make disciples of all nations' (28:19) although before his death he had been sent 'only to the lost sheep of the house of Israel' (15:24). Jesus had shared the traditional hope of Israel that one day 'many will come from east and west' – the 'many' including righteous Gentiles as well as dispersed Jews – to worship Israel's God (8:5–13). Now that boldly inclusive hope was being fulfilled and Matthew thought it right to include in his gospel a long passage about signs of the coming of 'the end of the age' before 'this generation' dies (24:3–31). But the inclusion was made some fifty years after the day when Jesus was said to have been teaching on the Mount of Olives and it seems obvious that a speech of this length, much longer than Mark's material and not in Q, had never been recorded at the time. It may, however, represent the teaching of at least one Christian prophet.

Luke's gospel (17:20, 21) says about the coming 'days of the Son of Man' that the final judgement will be as sudden and as obvious as a flash of lightning. But until then 'the kingdom of God is not coming with things that can be observed', for the kingdom of God is – what? The Greek word can mean either 'among you' or 'within' you, but the first meaning is almost certainly right because Jesus is speaking to Pharisees, whom he has criticised. His message demands a personal response but is more than personal, for what is being done can be pointed to in the image of Satan falling from heaven (10:18). By actions which his hearers can observe the power of evil is being destroyed.

The evidence provided by the gospels is therefore not simple and has aroused much debate, yet almost all the scholars are now agreed that the confusion is not total. That idea of God's royal rule was familiar to all Jews and Jesus used it in order to challenge people to accept this government in their own lives with a promise that what they accepted would be completed as noon follows dawn. Although he did not make his whole message depend on this hope being fulfilled, he did hope that after a 'time of trial' the transformation of life in the world he knew would follow quickly. Nothing less sensational than this hope can account for the excitement which he aroused or for the alarm of the authorities.

These authorities did not include the Pharisees (the 'Separated'), who thought that the common people ought to be as holy as they were. Nor were the scribes in power: they were laymen who, in addition to earning a living as clerks, were willing to expound the Scriptures which they could read. The gospels can easily leave the impression that the Pharisees and scribes were the chief enemies of Jesus. In particular Matthew's chapter 23 suggests that they had fallen into almost every temptation into which a teacher of religion or morality can fall. They do not practise what they preach; they do not help people to bear the burdens which they impose; they show off their status but do not earn it; they teach nonsense or triviality but neglect justice and mercy; they are hypocrites and children of hell. No doubt not all the Pharisees and scribes were saints, but this tirade was at least edited by Matthew at a time when relations between churches and synagogues were bitter.

The gospels contain evidence of friendly relationships with some Pharisees who invited Jesus to dinner and warned him about dangers (Luke 7:36, 13:31). No doubt they were shocked by some of his unconventional behaviour, although this never amounted to any major breach of the Jewish religious law and he seems to have attended a synagogue every Sabbath. They would have been distressed that he extended the concessions about Sabbath-keeping which were intended to provide for emergencies. When he healed someone who could have waited for a day, his explanation that the Sabbath was intended to benefit human well-being would have seemed dangerous in what it might imply (Mark 2:23–27). Equally suspect would be his radicalism if he really said that what defiles someone is what comes out of the mouth, not what enters it (Mark 7:15), because that saying opened up the prospect of all the Jews' food laws being abandoned after centuries of strict observance and Paul would have been very glad to use it during his own controversies about these laws. But controversy was a feature of the Judaism in this period and nothing which Jesus is known to have said or done was blasphemy under the religious law. In the gospels there is talk of stoning him in accordance with the law but this never happened.

The Jews who debated with this unusual teacher were not in power at this stage. Their time would come when both the temple and the nation had been destroyed after the disastrous rebellions. Then the Jewish people would have been in total despair had they not been given a clearly defined system of religious regulations, made more humane in some cases, as the definition and declaration of their continuing identity. The Christians had not joined the rebellion and would be regarded as traitors by Jews who had paid very heavily for their patriotism. Nor could they join in the reconstruction of Judaism; too many Gentiles were now in full membership of the Christian community. So they could no longer claim when it suited them to be one of the parties within Judaism, the group called the Nazarenes (as in Acts 24:5). All this explains the curse on the Nazarenes added to the eighteen Jewish 'benedictions' recited in synagogues. It also explains – without excusing – the bitterness which poisoned some passages in the gospels about the Jews and invented the fateful cry 'His blood be on us and on our children!' (Matthew 27:25).

In the lifetime of Jesus the only powerful Jews were those who owed their positions to collaboration with Romans. They would be determined to get rid of him – but not because his disciples did not wash their hands before meals (Mark 7:5), nor because he himself incurred greater impurity by going among tombs and pigs (Mark 7:5), but because the reason given for being eccentric was that a king who was not Caesar was about to set up a new kingdom. This was a time of many and varied hopes that the tragedies of Israel were about to end: somehow the temple made magnificent by Rome's puppet ruler would be made pure and the holy land cleansed from foreign rule. Since the Roman conquest in 63 BC these hopes had already inspired many rebellions including a big one in AD 6, followed by thousands of crucifixions. The carpenter's sensitive son in Nazareth, then probably about to enter his teens, would feel intensely both about the violence of the rebels and about the brutality of the victors. After a time of sullen silence more risings were to follow in AD 41, 52, 66 and 132, until Jerusalem was destroyed and rebuilt as a pagan city which Jews were forbidden to enter. In this atmosphere the accusation against Jesus which brought about this death was that he incited people to rebellion, not against the law of Moses but against the rule of Rome.

Mark, Matthew and Luke retained this 'kingdom' language because Jesus had used it despite its very dangerous associations. Indeed, Luke began his volume about the acts of the apostles with the disciples' question, 'Lord, is this the time when you will restore the kingdom to Israel?', and ended the book with Paul teaching about the kingdom of God in Rome itself. Such honesty about what had been the message of Jesus was risky and we can notice how the risk is avoided in the Gospel of Thomas outside the Bible. There, the promise is to the individual seeker after truth, who would eventually 'rule over all'. The 'kingdom' is a condition in which 'you know yourselves' and 'recognise what is before your eyes' (3, 5). On the way to that kingdom without God, prayer and fasting 'will bring sin on yourselves' (14, 104). This spirituality is for a spiritual elite, for one in a thousand (23). The lost sheep is valued here not because it is lost but because it is the biggest (107). Pilate would have thought the Jesus of Thomas no danger to Rome but a man out of this world and out of his mind.

Another problem facing the gospel-writers was that they wrote at a time when it had to be acknowledged that any hope that the kingdom of God would come quickly had not come true. They had also to admit that their Lord had shared this hope in ignorance. It was not for his disciples 'to know the times or periods that the Father has set by his own authority' (Acts 1:7) – but it was not for Jesus to know either. Mark has gathered predictions current among Christians about the End, and has included the assurance that 'this generation will not pass away until all these things have taken place' – but he then has to admit that 'about that day or hour no one knows, neither the angels in heaven, nor the Son but only the Father' (13:30, 32). The language about 'the Son', without explanation, suggests that this admission was phrased by the Christians themselves, but it shows that they would not defend a claim that their Lord accurately foresaw when that kingdom would come, any more than they would share the claim of Thomas Aquinas in the Middle Ages that Jesus knew that he was God. They knew that he was human.

So far from losing faith in Jesus, their Yes to him increased when the full coming of the kingdom he had proclaimed was postponed year by year – a very remarkable development. Belief in the imminent End was too strong to die quickly; indeed, it has never died out completely among Christians. The earliest surviving Christian document, Paul's letter to the church of the Thessalonians, showed how the coming of the End had been personalised into the second coming of Jesus. He declared as 'the word of the Lord' that 'we who are alive, who are left until the coming of the Lord', will join the resurrected 'dead in Christ' and 'meet the Lord in the air' (4:15–17). In Acts Peter interprets the phenomena of Pentecost as signs that 'the last days' have begun and the believers pool their possessions and spend 'much time' in the temple instead of going to work (2:43–47). The last of the books collected to form the New Testament repeats the prayer 'Our Lord, come!' and ends 'I, Jesus, surely am coming quickly'. But his letter to the Philippians (1:3–11, 20–24) shows that Paul lived to believe that for him the 'day of Christ' would probably be in heaven and most readers of the Revelation of John have come to value it mainly not for its detailed forecasts (which were inconsistent in their details) but for its visions of the risen Jesus and of the eternal City of God 'prepared as a bride for her husband' (1:18, 21:2). Such a faith could survive even when hopes of the imminent second coming of Jesus were repeatedly disappointed, for what mattered most was not when Jesus would 'come again', but what experienced facts had already shown him to be.

This development into what most of us know as Christianity was made possible because the self-effacement of Jesus as he had proclaimed his message had not been complete. As we have seen, the character of Jesus is visible even when he taught and worked in Galilee to proclaim God's power, not his own identity. But step by step he revealed much more of who he was in his most difficult and most characteristic decisions and deeds in Jerusalem – and that became the identity of the Christ of Christianity, Christ himself being the 'power of God' revealed in the midst of time, of evil and of defeat. Had he not moved into this second stage of his work, presumably he would now be

remembered – if at all – as one of the many teachers of hopes which
were illusions and as one of the healers of people who later died like
everyone else.

Surprisingly in view of what they are to say about him, the gospels
invite us to meet the adult Jesus as he stands wet in the river Jordan
among other Jews who have been convinced by John the Baptist's promise that they will escape imminent doom if they are immersed as a
sign of their repentance. They are self-confessed sinners but they need
not go to the temple in Jerusalem for a sacrifice, or even to one of the
baths for ritual cleansing to be found all over the country.

Luke believed that Jesus was 'about thirty years old' when baptised
and for a man of that age to place himself in this position indicates that
thoughts which had been building up for many years now exploded.
The gospels suggest this by saying that this carpenter heard a voice from
heaven calling him 'my beloved son': as the psalms showed, kings were
called that. Mark says that he now 'saw the heavens torn apart' (1:10),
but it is less spectacular to think that in this crisis he became intensely
convinced that he had been called by God to a mission.

It seems that John's gospel (1:19–42) was right to say that Jesus joined
John's mission as an assistant and met his own first disciples in that
circle. Mark (1:14) is clear that he did not begin his independent work
until after the Baptist's arrest, but Matthew (11:2–19) admits that
although very highly praised by Jesus, John did not understand him,
and it seems that at this stage the man from Nazareth did not even
understand himself and his own mission completely. These two gospels
reproduce the tradition that he withdrew for reflection into the desert,
balancing one memory of the Bible against another. Should he begin a
mission in which manna would be provided for him and his followers
as food from God, as it had been to Moses? Would he win applause by
dramatic miracles, trusting in the divine protection promised by at least
one psalm? Would he be a king in the ordinary sense? But he remembered the Bible's central message: humankind does not depend on
bread alone, God's power is not to be tested, at present the world is
under the power of evil but God alone is fully entitled to rule it.

A further 'time of trial' seems to be indicated in reports that this
carpenter-turned-missionary was rejected in his own village, that he
could not heal anyone there because there was no atmosphere of faith,
and that his family had to be told that he no longer belonged to them
(Mark 3:31–34, 6:1–6; Luke 4:16–30). In response he gathered a new
family, with his followers accepting similar partings, at least for a
mission likely to be brief: this is the background to the sayings that he
had come to set fire to the world and that villagers to whom family life

and honour had meant everything must 'hate father and mother, wife and children, brothers and sisters, yes and even life itself' (Luke 12:49, 14:26). Before long he organised the mission under the leadership of twelve men to represent the twelve tribes of Israel (Mark 3:13–9, 5:7–13). Opposition to his message had united some intensely patriotic Pharisees with the Herodians who supported Roman rule and the Sadducees who supported the Jerusalem temple under Roman patronage (Mark 12:13–18), but whatever became of Jesus, this community could survive his death.

It seems that he had not yet taught his disciples that his death was imminent. But Mark (8:27, 9:8) records a decisive time in which the leading disciples were told this, to their amazement. Now Jesus accepted that he would probably suffer the Roman punishment of crucifixion, warned his followers to 'take up' their own cross, and took Peter, James and John up a high mountain (probably Hermon) in order to pray about this terrible prospect. That March day turned out to be a time for communion not only with the Father but also with the saints, in particular with Moses and Elijah, representatives of the Law and Prophets in his heritage. They appeared in a 'vision' (Matthew 7:9) and Jesus became filled with light (a condition reported about some other mystics when in ecstasy). For some moments he was transfigured by the power which would take him to death and beyond.

So the tragedy is not what then lay ahead for him. It lies in much of the history of the Christian Church which, while taking his name and heaping on him devotional and theological praise unmatched in the history of the world, has not fully faced the question 'Why do you call me "Lord, Lord" and do not do what I tell you?' (Luke 6:46), and the warning 'Not everyone who says to me "Lord, Lord" will enter the kingdom of heaven but only the one who does the will of my Father in heaven' (Matthew 7:21). Tragically often, the God of the churches has been a God of power not love, and of wrath not mercy, and the clergy have been close to the rich and the respectable, not to the downtrodden and the outcasts, and not even using their access to power in order to support justice in society. The power of the state has been used to punish 'heretics' who have disagreed with orthodoxy about the enthroned Christ, but what Jesus actually was has been obscured. The Father of Jesus has been presented as the all-powerful Lord who takes care of those who praise him in the correct style, but who condemns the bulk of humankind to suffering and ignorance before death and to endless torment after it, without involving himself in the mess or sinking into the filth. As an Anglican, I think with shame about some of the history of the Church of England which became the state church under the monstrous Henry VIII, with the collaborating laymen occupying or pulling down the monasteries. Later, landowners appointed the clergy and compelled their tenants to attend the parish church while most of the senior clergy were blind to the extent of cruelty and corruption in a society which had given them rich and undemanding privileges. And no doubt this betrayal of Christ has been matched elsewhere.

The parables which Jesus told cannot be forgotten so easily but their sting has been removed by ignoring the fact that they were stories about the beginning of the transformation of the world in the kingdom of God, with laws about love accepted by love. The work of God the Healer, brought to some of the sick by Jesus as a sign of that kingdom's arrival, has been reduced to the spiritual rebirth of Christians and to miracles which sensationally contradict the normal processes of nature. Modern medical knowledge and skill have not always been connected with this kingdom's progress, as has also been true about much else in the increase in human knowledge and skill and in the humane treatment of humankind.

In history it has often been taught that the whole of the Bible is the Word of God, but in practice some bits of Scripture have always been thought more significant than others. A frequent error in the churches has been to choose the wrong bits, so that it might seem that in the wilderness Jesus ought to have chosen to be a king, and on the mountain he ought to have remembered what is said to have been a message to Moses from God: 'Go back and forth from gate to gate throughout the camp, and let each of you kill your brother, your friend and your neighbour' (Exodus 32:27). Perhaps also, as he faced his own enemies, he ought to have copied one action reported of Elijah, who had happily presided over the massacre of four hundred and fifty prophets of Baal (1 Kings 18:40)?

But through the centuries countless Christians have been wisely discriminating in their obedience to the Scriptures and have ignored or rejected some of the teachings and examples given by the official leaders of churches. They have lived and died with courage in the company of Jesus, inspired by his image of God as Abba and by images of his own personality based on the gospels and on the characters of Christlike saints. They have known that it was not the mission of Jesus to claim that God had already arranged the world (both nature and society) according to his own wishes, so that no complaints from the disadvantaged were acceptable. His message was that in his work God's reign had begun to arrive – and it was a message about a revolution in hearts and minds and consequently in society. In some hearts and minds that revolution has been a reality. That has made salt which the world can taste as something different, and light which people can see radiating from God, the Eternal and the Father (Matthew 5:13–16).

FOUR

~

YES TO HIS VICTORY

WHEN JESUS MADE his decision to go to a Jerusalem crowded and heavily policed during the Passover festival, it was a deliberate challenge to the religious and political authorities and he must have thought that probably his death would be the outcome. But he had already done what he could to challenge the people in Galilee to change their minds and lives as the coming of the kingdom of God was proclaimed by words and signs. Now he had to ask a wider representation of the people of Israel, gathered to celebrate deliverance from slavery in Egypt long ago, whether they would accept liberation from their continuing refusal to live according to the will of God.

According to his interpretation, that freedom-through-obedience would not be achieved by living according to the Jewish religious law when it was not fully humane: the supreme law is that God commands the love of humanity because he practises it himself. Nor would the freedom promised by Jesus include a miraculously rapid escape from Roman rule and poverty. It would mean escape from the self-destruction inevitable unless some momentous change in attitude ended the spiral of hatred, violence, punishment and revenge. This freedom from national suicide might be secured by a conversion of the Jews (and Romans?) or by a miracle on a cosmic scale, but he knew the facts of history and of his own time. Luke has his lament: 'it is impossible for a prophet to be killed outside Jerusalem. Jerusalem, Jerusalem – how often have I desired to gather your children together as a hen gathers her brood under her wings!' (13:31–35). And when he sees the city after his last journey to it, he weeps because it never knows 'the things that make for peace' (20:41–44).

We cannot know exactly what was going on in the mind of Jesus, which being human was probably a mixture of hopes and fears, of deliberate actions and brilliantly phrased teachings, with an unspoken uncertainty kept under control until a time in Gethsemane. But all the reliable evidence which we have is consistent with one interpretation: knowing that death might be very near, he decided to let go – to cease to control events and to let God act while he himself did what was right, whatever the consequences.

His public entry into Jerusalem was one of his great symbolic acts, the beginning of the climax of his mission to Israel. He did not walk into the city like an ordinary pilgrim: he rode, but on a young donkey as a sign that his was a mission of peace. Zechariah's prophecy about a king who would not enter Jerusalem on a dressed-up horse (9:9) was in the background. Probably only a few understood the symbolism and there were shouts of a different kind of welcome to 'the one who comes in the name of the Lord' to restore 'the kingdom of our ancestor David', with the cry *Hosanna*, which means 'save now' (Mark 11:9, 10). But he had no ambition to be the general of an army to liberate Israel from the Romans. According to Luke (19:45, 46) his immediate purpose was to demonstrate in the temple, specifically in the Court of the Gentiles, that the kingdom of God was open to all without any payment other than a change of heart.

In Mark's gospel (11:15–19) he has a night's rest after walking from Galilee (which would take a week), but not before he has 'looked around at everything'. Then 'he began to drive out those who were selling and those who were buying' in what was intended to be 'a house of prayer for all nations'. In particular he 'overturned the tables of the money changers and the seats of those who sold doves'. And 'the whole crowd was spellbound'. This action which sealed his fate was of course symbolic: no doubt order was soon restored and normal business resumed. But a great deal was implied. The temple should not be the symbol of nationalism and of clerical power, nor should it reek with the blood of animals slaughtered in the belief that such sacrifices were needed to make sure of God's blessing. All that was needed was heartfelt and humble prayer by Jew or Gentile, amid quiet, not this racket. In particular Jesus protested against the charade which was designed to increase the wealth of the priests controlling the temple: coins bearing the Roman emperor's head might be used every day by Jews, and brought into the temple, but must be exchanged (at a fee) for the coinage of Tyre, stamped with an inoffensive palm tree, if God was to be pleased by the purchase of an animal to be killed. And his fury was aroused by the insistence that even the poorest must pay for a bird.

Next morning he was asked about his authority to cause such a disturbance, and replied that priests who had not acknowledged the prophetic authority of the Baptist would not be able to understand him (11:23–33). Later he watched a widow putting two small copper coins into the collection box, leaving herself unable to pay for food that day, and he said that this was better worship than all the sacrifices by people who could well afford the expense (12:41–44).

Rebellious slogans as he rode into the city had been dangerous, but if the Roman garrison heard of that incident no action had been taken; small-scale overexcitement could be overlooked. This public insult to the authorities of the temple was far more serious and they had to retaliate. It makes sense to think that they now looked for an opportunity to make an arrest which would not cause a riot, and that they planned to report Jesus to the Roman governor as a political rebel, which would make sure that his punishment would be the prolonged agony of a rebel's death. In AD 62 another high priest was to have Jesus' brother James stoned to death, almost certainly because he too had criticised the temple's rich clergy, although he was well known to be strict in keeping the religious law. Before that, this was to be the fate of the first Christian martyr, an outspoken critic of the temple (Acts 7). But it would be controversial to stone a man so popular as Jesus and even if a hostile mob could be assembled, or a murder arranged, a quick death would not be suitable for a man so dangerous.

He increased the danger by returning to the temple to teach, as any Jew was entitled to do. The gospels show the kind of thing he said, but the chief provocation was his accurate prediction, reported in a number of versions, that the magnificent architecture, provided by King Herod to advertise that brutal ruler's piety, would be totally destroyed if the Jews ceased to consent to Roman supremacy as Herod had done. But that would not matter greatly, for a purer temple would be built and Jesus had already shown what should have the priority over any ritual intended as magic to secure God's favour. If you remember that someone has a grievance against you, leave the sacrificial animal before the altar until you have been reconciled with 'your brother' (Matthew 5:23, 24). The purer temple, with or without stones, would be built by sinners who have forgiven each other and then turned to God as 'Abba! Father!'

Mark believed that the last supper was the Passover meal, carefully arranged beforehand because Jesus knew that he would never drink wine again 'until that day when I drink it new in the kingdom of God' (14:12–25). That left a major miracle, the coming of the kingdom, as a possible alternative to death but Luke saw no ambiguity: this was the 'Passover before I suffer' (22:15). And the symbolic actions reported by Mark signified not only that this was a special occasion (wine was not drunk at ordinary meals except by the rich) but also that a new 'covenant' was being made between God and 'many' (which often implied 'all'). It was the custom to sacrifice an animal in order to mark a solemn agreement between Jews, recalling the tradition that oxen had been sacrificed when God and Israel had concluded a treaty in the time of Moses (Exodus 24:5–8). The new covenant was to be made after a human return to obedience to God as demanded and predicted by Jeremiah (31:31–34), and it seems clear that Jesus had decided (recently?) that his own role was to provide the sacrifice – his own life. He expressed this conviction by giving signs which the other Jews gathered around him at Passover would understand very well.

According to Mark (14:22–25) Jesus took the loaf, tore it and gave it to his disciples with the simple words 'Take, this is my body'; later he passed round a cup of wine with 'This is my blood of the new covenant, poured out for many.' To Mark (10:45) this would signify the body and lifeblood being given 'as a ransom for many', to buy freedom as the Mosaic covenant-with-sacrifice had been made at the time of Israel's liberation from Egypt – and this ransom would be paid 'instead of' many payments which the liberated were in no position to offer.

Luke (21:19, 20) adds a command to repeat these actions: 'Do this in remembrance of me.' He also makes a small change in the words over the cup: 'This cup that is poured out for you is the new covenant in my blood', indicating more clearly that the death is the sacrifice made in order to have the treaty. And Matthew (26:28) adds that the blood is poured out for many 'for the forgiveness of sins', as Israel's sins had been forgiven at the time of the Mosaic covenant. These gospels may have been so phrased in reply to rumours that the Christians were cannibals, or laments that they flouted the Jewish law against eating meat from which the blood had not been drained. It was important to teach what Christians did believe: they solemnly commemorated a holy Lord and the bread and wine symbolised his life and death because these had made a new relationship with God possible.

But we know that these damaging rumours and laments were rife later, and we can think it likely that the Christians would not have continued to expose themselves to such attacks, had not their Lord commanded the repetition. They paid a price for repeating actions which then (as later) could be misunderstood outside their original setting.

In his first letter to Corinth (11:17–34) Paul had, it seems, already responded to misunderstandings. He had insisted that he had received the story of the last supper 'from the Lord' (but without explaining how) and he had used words almost identical with those in Luke's later account, avoiding any idea that blood was to be drunk physically. He also rebuked any thought that the meal around these actions, now re-enacted in a Greek port, would be an excuse for a party where 'one goes hungry and another becomes drunk'. The solemn purpose was to proclaim 'the Lord's death until he comes'. But the precise words of Jesus were, it seems, not always remembered: his actions were what mattered, and it had to be hoped that they would be given a thoughtful understanding in Corinth, a place which could scarcely have been more different from Jerusalem.

There was not even a complete agreement between Christians about the precise date of the last supper. Most scholars are now agreed that it is unlikely that it was held as nightfall marked the beginning of the Passover festival and was quickly followed by the arrest, interrogation and crucifixion. Neither the Jewish nor the Roman authorities would have risked the public execution while religious and patriotic enthusiasm was at its height. Mark says that the plot 'to arrest Jesus by stealth and kill him' had begun some days previously, with the intention of avoiding a riot that might result from an arrest in public or an execution on the festival (14:1–2, 10–11). Jesus must have been aware of the mounting hostility, so that time was short and he wanted to be sure of a final meal where at least the atmosphere would belong to Passover. It seems significant, however, that in these gospels no mention is made of a performance of the ceremonies which belonged to the Passover tradition: here was something new.

John's gospel says that during his public life Jesus had already attended two Passover festivals (2:23, 6:4), and previous visits to Jerusalem are probable, both because he was a devout Jew and because the other gospels suggest that he was already known in the city. But John is clear that this meal, the arrest and the death were 'before the festival of the Passover' (13:1). This agrees with the statement by an enemy among the Jews that the execution of this 'magician' had been on the eve of the festival. But John's account does not draw attention to his own time for the death, on the day when the lambs needed for sacrifice were slaughtered in the temple. It says only that Jesus was crucified on 'the day of preparation' before 'a day of great solemnity' which was also a Sabbath (19:31). This would make the date 7 April 30.

In keeping with a downplaying of the Passover-sacrifice theme, this gospel includes a lengthy version of the teaching at the supper without making it clear that what was done then was the origin of the Eucharist. Although his language is shaped by unspoken knowledge about the last supper, for the Jesus of John the need to 'eat my flesh and drink my blood' is primarily a need to be fed spiritually by 'food which comes down from heaven' (6:27–59). He makes this point by what is described – the humble washing of the disciples' feet, so that they will 'do as I have done to you' (13:7–15). In John's mind, it seems, this implies an intimacy of love within the community which eats and drinks spiritual life, but in the conscience of many Christians the act has also been understood as a command to wash the feet of the world.

The disciples who had been at the supper carried daggers for self-defence (were they not countrymen in a city?) and according to Luke 6:15 the group included Simon 'the Zealot' – which may have meant more than 'the Enthusiast', for later rebels were to be called Zealots. Another disciple was Judas 'Iscariot' and whatever may have been his motive in his own eyes the Christian tradition was that this traitor was simply bribed. He ran from the supper to the temple police with information about where they could make a quiet arrest, the garden of Gethsemane at the foot of the Mount of Olives. When they arrived Jesus stopped any resistance; he had recovered his calm through prayer after a short time of fear and uncertainty. The disciples all fled unheroically and Peter brought shame on himself when he attempted to observe events anonymously and, in panic when spotted, had to deny knowing Jesus. All these events sound genuine, for gospel-writers would not have invented stories which suggest cowardice.

Jesus was interrogated by the controllers of the temple although Mark (14:53–65) was mistaken to think of this as a formal trial by the council, the Sanhedrin, for that would have been doubly illegal: no trial could be held by night or during a festival. But the accused seems to have thought that any defence would be useless in the face of determined hostility and later Christians, who would not have been present, may well have been told this. Mark thought that when challenged directly by the high priest Jesus did at last admit that he was the 'anointed' (*mashiah*) king, although even then he preferred the non-military image of the Son of Man. Matthew and Luke thought that he did not answer the question. Other men were to claim to be the Messiah in the next hundred years, but that in itself was not a sin punishable by death under Jewish law. That would also apply to any ambiguous claim to be 'Son of Man' or 'Son of God'. The crucial points were that Jesus could not deny having publicly attacked the management of the temple and did not make enough private concessions to avoid being taken to the Roman governor as a troublemaker who was at least a potential leader of a rebellion.

Pilate was a man notorious for being too cruel even by Roman standards; non-Christian sources (Josephus and Philo) report this, and he was to be sacked for it in AD 37. He may well have hesitated in this case because by all accounts Jesus was no ordinary criminal, and it is possible that some pressure had to be applied by the priests and the little crowd accompanying them, probably composed of people who owed their living to the temple, while most citizens and all pilgrims would be busy with the preparations for the festival. He would have been as impatient as another governor, Gallio, who in Acts refuses to be troubled by 'questions about words and names and your own law'

(18:15). But even a Roman official with a softer character would have been highly unlikely to take the risk of releasing a troublemaker reported by priests collaborating with Rome to have attacked them in public, and to have talked often about a kingdom where Caesar would not be supreme – a man, moreover, who did not deny those charges. Jesus was promptly crucified along with two bandits, under a little placard with the sneer 'King of the Jews'. This was in an abandoned quarry just outside the city wall.

The gospels agree that some women who had followed him were allowed to watch the terrible scene and Mark (15:21) says that a passer-by was conscripted to carry the beam on which the exhausted man was to be tied or nailed down while his feet were nailed to a little platform on the upright beam to await death, which usually came slowly through pain and suffocation. The unwilling helper, Simon of Cyrene, was 'the father of Alexander and Rufus' who were known to Mark's readers as Christians: presumably he had been converted by what he saw and reported. But both Mark (5:34) and Matthew (27:46) say that as Jesus died he quoted from Psalm 22: 'My God, my God, why have you for-saken me?' – and they report no other word. Presumably these gospel-writers wished to show that he had shared to the full the physical and mental agony of the Christian martyrs and of the Jewish martyrs whose ordeals had probably inspired that psalm, but it is extremely unlikely that they would have put such a cry into the mouth of their Lord had they not believed that as a matter of history it had come from their Lord's heart. Many more hopeful passages of Scripture could have been quoted, including much of this psalm.

Luke (23:26–49) preferred other stories, probably also already treasured by Christians but not for that reason incredible as history. On his way to the cross Jesus had told women to weep for themselves, not for him, because one day the now inevitable rebellion against Rome would be a total disaster, when mothers would envy women who had no children to be killed. As the nails were driven into his body he had soaked up the hatred and the violence like a sponge, praying aloud for the executioners who 'do not know what they are doing'. (But this is not in all the ancient manuscripts.) He had promised Paradise to the fellow victim who despite his crimes showed a glimmer of understanding. Finally he had quoted from Psalm 3: 'Father, into your hands I commend my spirit.'

Whatever was actually said then amid the excruciating pain, none of these 'words from the cross' is out of keeping with the character of Jesus as known from evidence about his previous life. When they recovered from their grief and despair, Christians could say truly that the agony belonged to a spiritual triumph. They could see that Jesus had never been closer to the Father than when in his service he suffered so much that he felt deserted and without any explanation. The teacher and storyteller of the joy of God's kingdom had been covered by the depths of physical and mental pain, and while there had set the supreme example of the power of courage, forgiveness and sympathy. The martyr condemned by religious and political power had ended his mission as a companion of the outcasts, yet in blind faith had remained God's prime minister. He had taught by living and dying and had gone home with his work done, to Abba in Paradise.

The Proclaimer of the Kingdom became the Proclaimed as his story was told to the centuries and the continents, and every human talent has been employed in praise. But even in the praise there has always been a human element, and it was so at the beginning. In the style of their time these gospels erect banners to celebrate this victory, in the shape of legends. Mark tells of an earthquake, of a prolonged eclipse of the sun, and of a split from top to bottom in the curtain guarding the holiest shrine in the temple. Matthew tells of many tombs bursting open then and many 'saints' being seen alive when Jesus had been 'raised' himself. And there may be a legend when Luke says that the centurion in charge of the execution concluded that the man was innocent; in Mark the tribute was to 'God's son'. Solid evidence suggests, unsurprisingly, that the cause of Jesus seemed to be buried with him. From a strictly historical viewpoint, the evidence about how Jesus himself was buried seems not completely solid, however. According to Mark (15:42–46) the 'respected' Joseph of Arimathea risked being accused of complicity with the claim of Jesus to be 'king' when he obtained permission from Pilate to take down the body, wrap it in a cloth, and bury it in a tomb. According to Matthew (27:57–66) next day Pilate was told that Jesus had promised to 'rise again' and therefore ordered the tomb to be guarded. According to John (19:38–42) Joseph was accompanied by another secret disciple, Nicodemus a leading Pharisee, and together they wrapped a very large amount of spices around the body. The signs of veneration for the crucified Jesus are mounting and if 'John' is being imaginative when he gives us a long conversation between Jesus and Nicodemus in his chapter 3, it seems possible that devoutly Christian traditions are historically unreliable here and that the atmosphere of desolated mourning is better conveyed when we are told that a few women later brought a few spices in order to reduce the stench of the corpse's decay, so that the tomb could be used again in the near future (Mark 16:1).

A series of events followed which were essential to the rise of Christianity and therefore now demand detailed and fearless discussion. Undeniably it is more convenient when the question about the resurrection of Jesus as an historical fact is not explored – when the stories about it are simply accepted as sacred, or when they are loved with the qualification that the facts behind them cannot be known now, or when the question is not taken seriously because it is thought to be obvious that the death of Jesus was the end of his life although not of his influence. But his resurrection is so central in the New Testament that every moral and intellectual effort ought to be put into a search for the truth about it. Even if the search upsets others or one's own deepest feelings, and even if the result can still be contradicted, perhaps within one's own fallible mind, one must cling to the truth that God wants truth.

The gospels say that women came to the tomb very early on the day after the Sabbath. This first day of the week in the Jewish calendar was soon to replace the Sabbath as the Christians' holy day; when in his first letter Paul reminded Corinthians of their duty to put money aside 'on the first day of every week' (16:2), or when a Christian wrote that 'I was in the Spirit on the Lord's day' (Revelation 1:10), he would be understood. It therefore seems reasonable to conclude that for Christians a supremely important event had occurred one Sunday.

But who were these women? At Mark 16:1 'Mary Magalene and Mary the mother of James and Salome'; at Matthew 28:1 'Mary Magdalene and the other Mary'; at Luke 24:1 'the women who had come with him from Galilee'; and at John 20:1 only Mary Magalene. It is impressive that only women are mentioned, for at the time they were not trusted as witnesses – so they may be cited here because they really were there. But it is not agreed exactly who they were. In the absence of a story with agreed details, it seems reasonable to say that when slightly different stories were told the details were not remembered accurately.

How did they hope to enter the tomb to anoint the corpse (their motive for Mark and Luke) if they expected to find a great stone rolled over the entrance? We are not told, but they may have come to mourn outside and may have intended to wait until men came who would be willing to move the great stone. If they found that the stone was already rolled away, or (according to Matthew 28:2) saw an angel doing this, why did they find the tomb empty – if they did? The explanation of this miracle is said to have been given by a supernatural message. For Mark, 'a young man, dressed in a white robe, and sitting' on a ledge in the tomb, tells the three women that 'he has been raised; he is not here. Look, there is the place where they laid him. But go, tell his disciples and Peter that he is going ahead of you to Galilee; there you will see him, just as he told you' (16:5–7). But who this 'young man' is we are not told, and for Matthew the messenger is an angel 'descending from heaven' and looking 'like lightning', with clothing 'white as snow' (28:2–3). For Luke, 'two men in dazzling clothes' do not tell the women that the disciples must go to Galilee; they remind them that 'while he was still in Galilee' he had promised that he would 'rise again' (24:4–7). Evidently there was no single Christian tradition to be recorded in any detail and we are at liberty to ask about the truth.

The story that his disciples stole and reburied the body was reported by Matthew (28:11–15) to be 'still told among the Jews to this day', but it passes belief that the disciples were such confident and accomplished actors that having done this they quickly announced the supreme miracle and persisted in the pretence until their deaths (which might be martyrdoms). Mary Magdalene is said to have thought that a gardener had removed the body soon after the burial (John 20:15), but it is very unlikely that such an employee would have had a sufficiently strong motive to do something so contrary to any regulation or moral code. In modern times it has been suggested that the women had gone to the wrong tomb, but it is not likely that they would have been so muddled about a matter so close to their hearts. There has even been a theory that perhaps Roman executioners had not made sure that Jesus was dead. So all these attacks on Scripture may be dismissed.

However, many defences of the faith that the resurrection was physical depend on accepting the timetable found in the gospels, and about that there may be some scepticism.

Almost everyone who has spoken or written for the public about this question has done so in the profound conviction that the empty tomb is at the centre of the Christian faith, and has been so since the first Easter. Hearing or reading sincere and eloquent believers, probably with a deep respect for their lives and brains as well as for their positions in the Church, even people normally inclined to be sceptical can forget how extraordinary is the claim being made – that a corpse was completely dematerialised and then recreated without being subject to the limitations which accompany physicality, in an event announced by 'angels' who do seem to be physical. Or at least scepticism may be suppressed or silenced for a time, as may be the polite reaction when a believer witnesses to this faith strongly and perhaps passionately. But there has often been another reaction in societies where Christianity is eccentric or where free thought and free speech are common: there may be wonder, silent or expressed, that anyone can be so dishonest, stupid or self-deluded as to give voice to such an incredible faith. So it has become essential to ask carefully whether belief in a physical resurrection is really essential if there is to be faith that Jesus was raised from the dead. For many years I believed that it is, but I have come to see that a strong case may be made for another interpretation both of the evidence and of Christian faith.

The earliest surviving written evidence supporting this belief was, it seems, in Mark's gospel, compiled in Rome some forty years after the burial in Jerusalem: therefore any investigation must explore a period about which there can be little, if any, certainty. On the one hand, if the claim was made very soon after the burial, there is no evidence that it was refuted by the production of a body which had not been revived. Nor is it known that the claim was abandoned by anyone making it amid hostility and danger. These factors count in favour of the miracle's authenticity, as does the unusual use of women as witnesses. On the other hand, it is said that the miracle was not made fully public; no one witnessed the actual resurrection and at first no one believed it except a small number of people who had already become disciples. They persuaded some others but in the Acts of the Apostles (probably written some fifty or sixty years later) the persuasion is not done by any invitation to visit the empty tomb.

Within two or three years such an invitation would have been pointless, for the Jews had developed the custom of collecting and keeping the clean bones in a stone box (an ossuary) and their identity could then be known only by a name on the box. Normally the box was kept in the tomb but within fifteen years the area around the crucifixion was incorporated into the city, when presumably the tomb was closed permanently. But even the original burial in a tomb is not a certainty from a strictly historical viewpoint. Crucified people could be given the honour of a decent burial: the bones of one such, with a nail through the ankle, were recently discovered by archaeologists. But normally the Romans could be expected to deny this privilege to criminals on whom they had already inflicted extreme degradation, and in Jerusalem dishonoured corpses would be thrown with other rubbish into a pit in the Valley of Hinnom full of fire and lime and providing the biblical imagery of hell.

Such possibilities are offensive to Christians including myself, but the search for truth requires that they should be faced with honesty as well as sensitivity, instead of trying to win an argument that the historical evidence alone makes the emptiness of the tomb either certain or highly probable. On this evidence, it seems probable that on this distant Sunday visions of the risen Lord were seen, but that we cannot know more for certain. In this situation it is encouraging that the greatest of all evangelists, Paul, is not known ever to have claimed that the tomb in which Jesus was buried was emptied. What he believed had become of his Lord's mortal body when he was 'raised' we do not know if we are confined to his teaching which has survived. In this respect he may be called the patron saint of agnostics.

Two things seem certain about the stories of how Jesus 'appeared' after his death. They are some of the most beautiful and moving stories ever told – which is some evidence that some events inspired these writers to reach such heights. But their details are inconsistent and not easy to accept as accurate reporting, so that it is possible that these stories about the 'new creation' resemble the myths about the old creation at the beginning of the Bible – myths which communicate spiritual truth about spiritual experiences. It need not be thought that Christianity must be buried if modern people, very conscious of the need to test claims about physical events by the standards of the natural sciences and modern work in history, do not take the Easter stories literally any more than they take the first chapters of Genesis literally. The faith that 'Jesus is Lord' although he was dead could still be strong were it to be thought probable by most Christians that the bones of his mortal body remained in his tomb and were placed with reverence in an ossuary more than thirty years before the writing of the earliest of our gospels, and that what then became of them cannot be known.

Mark's gospel ends very strangely and much discussion has not produced a totally convincing explanation. We are told that the women were instructed to tell the disciples that they would see Jesus in Galilee, but 'they said nothing to anyone, for they were afraid' (16:8, with all surviving manuscripts written before the fifth century ending at the Greek word translated as 'for', which is odd but not unique). Probably Mark thinks of them as being bewildered and overawed by their mysterious experience, and as expecting to be treated as hysterical women, for mere nervousness about the authorities or the disciples scarcely accounts for this failure by women devoted to Jesus. Earlier the gospel has made clear Mark's belief that Jesus was raised from the dead as he had predicted, and this passage implies a belief that the women did after all tell their story about a vision to someone at some point, so why does he not end with an account of how the risen Jesus did himself appear to the disciples, either together despite the women's failure to gather them in a hurry, or individually?

It has been suggested that Mark thought that the Lord's only appearance would be at the imminent end of history, but when he wrote many years had already passed and he made the message given to the women sound urgent. It has also been suggested that he told how the Lord had appeared but that the end of the scroll, or of the last page in a book, was torn off before any copy had been made. But this too seems unlikely since the scroll or book would have been valued very highly and if damaged would have been either repaired or replaced. And copies with a proper end would surely have been made in time to reach Matthew and Luke, who would have felt obliged to reproduce Mark's version of a story so sacred.

Two suggestions (which so far as I know have not been made previously) may deserve consideration, although they can be no more than speculations. One is that the gospel was written in order to be read out in portions before a sermon. It was written for a church which was preoccupied by the possibility that some or many of its members would soon be called to become martyrs. Repeatedly the gospel stresses the call to share death by crucifixion in some way, along with the anxiety and fear resulting, before saying plainly that Jesus himself died in agony and despair and that his first followers showed no courage, and not even much intelligence. Such a gospel would reach the hearts and minds of fearful Christians who would, however, now hear a preacher's proclamation of the Lord's triumph and would participate in the dramatic enactment of death-and-triumph in the Eucharist.

Another suggestion is that the failure of the women did indeed prevent the quick gathering of the disciples in Galilee so that Jesus might appear to them together – but did not prevent smaller appearances in Jerusalem. As we shall see, this would fit the gospels of Luke and John, and this might well be what a preacher would have told Mark's church. However, the longest ending which was to be added to his gospel shows how fast and how far a Christian writer could fall from the level of the earliest years. Up to 16:8 the gospel is austere but not unsympathetic: it presents the disciples as being understandably confused and frightened and gives us a picture of Peter in tears (15:72). But the ending which was added presents a Jesus who first 'upbraided' the disciples and then promised them unfailing magical powers, while anyone who does not believe what they say departs to a final damnation. This is different from the encouragement of martyrs on their way to cruel deaths.

Matthew gives stories of two appearances. One was near the tomb, to women who were full of 'great joy' as well as fear. Suddenly Jesus appeared and repeated the angel's message. Then he appeared again, in Galilee as promised, to 'the eleven disciples' on a mountain. There he was worshipped but 'some doubted'. He told them that 'all authority in heaven and on earth' had been given to him and that they must 'go and make disciples of all nations', baptising them in the name of the Holy Trinity. It is impressive to see that a worldwide mission was accepted, and that belief in God as Trinity was already beginning, when this gospel was written well within Christianity's first century – but doubts about historical authenticity have at least one strong basis: Paul would have valued these words of the risen Jesus very highly but evidently they

were unknown to him as he advocated a controversial mission to the
Gentiles with baptism which was not explictly trinitarian. It is also the
case that in Acts baptism is 'in the name of Jesus Christ' only (as at 1:37)
and when extended to Gentiles (as at 10:48) causes surprise.

And a greater puzzle about Mark's and Matthew's gospels is why it
was divinely allowed that the historical evidence should be left in this
state if it was divinely willed that the whole Church should be confident
in faith in the 'bodily resurrection' of its Lord, involving a strong
physical element. The evidence would have been stronger had Mark and
Matthew ended with an Easter proclamation making it clear that in
these early years there was agreement about what the women found in
the tomb and what the disciples then experienced. But as it is, again we
seem to be entitled to be uncertain about the facts.

It seems that in this period the Pharisees taught, and most Jews
believed (although the Sadducees did not), that at the general resurrection of the dead, as history ends, some scriptural promises would be
fulfilled somehow. Such were 'Your dead shall live, their corpses shall
rise. O dwellers in the dust, awake and sing for joy!' (Isaiah 26:19); and
'Many of those who sleep in the dust of the earth shall awake, some to
everlasting life, and some to shame and everlasting contempt' (Daniel
12:2). 'Resurrection' interpreted in this strongly imaginative way had
been thought to be the only reward fit for martyrs (2 Maccabees 7), and
even when the hope was for 'immortality' it was believed that the
righteous must be given a visible triumph, imagined vividly (Wisdom
of Solomon 3—5). But there is no evidence of any expectation that anyone would be 'raised from the dead' in a physical sense before 'the end
of the age' meaning the end of normal history. Although it has often
been claimed that Paul must have understood 'raised from the dead' in
this sense, it does not seem likely that all intelligent and educated Jews
always took crudely physical imagery literally. In the Revelation of John
that overwhelmingly eloquent prophet cannot have done, for there is so
much imagery that it is impossible to reduce his imagination to a tidy
forecast of coming events. We may even ask whether 'Luke' intended
that everything in his presentation of this one resurrection within
history should be taken as 'history' in the modern sense.

To our great advantage, he is a storyteller. He tells of three appearances, all in or near Jerusalem, not in Galilee, and all during one day,
although in his second volume (Acts) there are to be forty days to make
provision for many 'instructions' including an order not to leave
Jerusalem until after the day of Pentecost. One of the appearances is to
Peter, but no account of it is given. Another is on the road to Emmaus,
where Jesus speaks at length about biblical references to the Messiah but
is recognised only when he breaks the bread at supper. At his third

appearance Jesus eats fish in the presence of his disciples before rising into the air from the Mount of Olives. These stories are told with great skill and countless Christians (including myself) have found them greatly significant, yet when thought about they become open to down-to-earth questioning.

The body of the risen Lord is said to have been one of 'flesh and bones', able to digest a meal, so how could it ascend into the clouds? And why did the disciples on the road not recognise that this was Jesus talking at length about biblical references to himself? The story implies that this body was clothed normally, but how had these clothes been obtained? Above all, Luke's gospel sharpens the question about how a body with many normal characteristics could appear and disappear at will. So the uncertainty about the resurrection being in some sense physical can remain for those whose minds are questioning by habit.

Fascination with the details in the biblical stories can result in our not noticing the gaps in what we are told. Nowhere in the gospels is there a story about what to Paul is the first appearance and presumably therefore the most astonishing and decisive – the one to Peter, whose position in the Church is to be of the highest importance in the future. Nor is it said what was the message to James the brother of Jesus, who was to take over the leadership in the mother-church, in Jerusalem. 'John' allocates the priority not to Peter or James but to Mary of Magdala; however, he tells us nothing else about her except that she had watched the crucifixion, while 'Luke' is tantalising when he mentions that Jesus had expelled seven demons from her (8:2). Paul is equally brief in his mention of the appearance to five hundred, without any explanation of how the risen Lord was 'seen' by so many. (Did some in the group 'doubt' as at Matthew 28:17, and if so why?) And he never puts on record a vivid account of the appearance which decided his own life.

Nor is any story told about an appearance of the risen Lord to his mother and his other brothers, although one seems possible if Acts 1:14 is right to report their presence among the apostles at a very early stage. The first volume by 'Luke' names Cleopas (24:18) alongside another disciple, and may imply that he received the first appearance, but we are not told why they were walking to Emmaus, or whether they were married, or who he was. The epilogue to the fourth gospel puts the beloved disciple in the background without saying whether or not Jesus spoke to him. Paul greets Andronicus and Junia, who presumably are married, as 'prominent among the apostles', having been 'in Christ before I was', and now they are leaders in the church in Rome (16:7). The Greek *apostolos* usually meant no more than 'envoy' or 'missionary', but both in Paul's letters and in the Acts of the Apostles it almost always refers to leaders with a special authority after a special closeness to Jesus, so that it seems possible that there had been an Easter appearance to this 'prominent' couple about whom we know nothing.

It seems possible to draw conclusions from these silences – that it was not intended to make the evidence as convincing as possible, and that most of those who received appearances were reticent about them and about other parts of their lives. The supreme example of modesty is Mary the mother of Jesus, who disappears from the Bible after Acts 1:14 and is referred to as 'a woman' by Paul (Galatians 4:4). She must have 'treasured all these things in her heart' (Luke 2:51) but she did not exhibit them. Evidently Scripture's witness to the resurrection was not inspired in order to satisfy our curiosity and does not encourage us to insist on details being accurate. Instead it suggests that what mattered supremely was the simple experience of 'seeing' and therefore 'knowing' Jesus as the risen Lord, an experience which united people so diverse as Peter and Paul, James and Mary, Cleopas, Junia and hundreds more. And the most important piece of evidence for the authenticity of the experience was, as Paul told the Corinthians, this: 'by the grace of God I am what I am' (1 Corinthians 15:10) because of a light shining in the heart which had given 'the knowledge of the glory of God in the face of Jesus Christ' (2 Corinthians 4:6).

It therefore appears inevitable that many modern-minded people to whom awkward questions occur do not forget them quickly and do not think it completely honest to keep quiet about them when instructed that in order to be Christians they must believe in the 'bodily' resurrection. They seem to be entitled by the present state of the evidence to believe, rather, that Jesus was indeed raised from death and defeat by the power of God, and that he was indeed seen in his triumphant glory by visions in the minds of women and men who had previously been heartbroken and in despair. Those experiences are 'facts' like many other 'facts' in generally accepted history: they are not absolutely certain but are highly probable and the evidence may rightly be thought sufficient for practical purposes.

It may also seem sensible to think that in addition to the actual resurrection of Jesus by the eternal God, and the visions of it, other facts inspired the stories told in the gospels. The early Christians must have owed much to evangelists who had previously been strangers, must have thought about the Hebrew Bible in a new light, and must have broken bread and shared wine in the Eucharist with a new insight. When they had other meals together they must have felt Christ's presence in the fellowship, and when they felt close to him in prayer they must also have felt that he was lifted above them in eternal majesty. And as their mission to all nations expanded they baptised converts so that these too might know the power of God as the Creator, as the Saviour and as the Spirit revealing new truth and enabling new life. In a vitally important sense, all this transforming experience was one big miracle.

The earliest, and for an historian the safest, evidence is found in Paul's letters. He did not tell any story about an appearance, presumably because he had no need to persuade his fellow Christians that their Lord had been raised, the words and lives of the missionaries having been sufficient evidence. Nor did he say anything about the empty tomb, presumably because if he knew of it he did not think it vitally important. But his whole life had been changed by an appearance to him in a vision, it seems within two or three years of the crucifixion. He reminded the Thessalonians that Jesus 'rose again' (4:14) and told the Galatians that 'God was pleased to reveal his son in me' (1:16). These are the earliest references, from about AD 50, but the Galatians were given his memory of a fortnight in Jerusalem about AD 35 in order to meet Peter and James and listen to their own experiences. In his first letter to Corinth (1:16–20) he recalled passing on what he had learned from them but he stressed that for three years he had been virtually on his own as he waited before seeking information: what mattered most to him was the revelation 'in' him. It mattered partly because his position in the Church depended entirely on it. He told the Galatians (1:1, 12) that he was an apostle because of direct action by 'Jesus Christ and God the Father who raised him from the dead'; he had not been taught the gospel which he now preached but had 'received it through a revelation of Jesus Christ'.

The list which he repeated in his first surviving letter to the Corinthians (15:3–8) was introduced by the simple statement 'that Christ was buried, and that he was raised on the third day in accordance with the scriptures'. That claim certainly accords with the frequently repeated promise in the Hebrew Bible that God will eventually triumph, but there are problems about the relevance of some passages which the early Christians are known to have quoted. In Psalm 16:10 it was read that 'You do not give me up to Sheol, or let your faithful one see the Pit' – but that seems to mean that the psalmist will not to be banished to the land of the dead on this occasion. At Hosea 6:2 it was read that 'on the third day he will raise us up' – but that is a part of a call to Israel and Judah to repeat when they have been 'struck down' by the Lord. If they do so, they will 'live before' him. It would seem that there was no detailed connection between the Hebrew Scriptures and the facts as stated in this letter with the passionate conviction that 'if Christ has not been raised . . . your faith has been in vain . . . we are even found to be misrepresenting God . . . you are still in your sins . . . those who have died in Christ have perished . . . we are of all people most to be pitied' (15:14–18). So we must ask what the facts were to Paul.

His list of 'appearances' is presented as a list of events. The risen Lord had appeared to Peter, to more than five hundred followers at once (many of them still alive when Paul wrote), and to his brother James. A second little list begins with an appearance to 'the Twelve' (had Judas been replaced, or had Paul forgotten about him?) and continues with one to 'all the apostles' (presumably a wider group). And it ends with an appearance to Paul alone, 'as to one untimely born'.

It seems that it had been thought that the appearances had ended but his experience was put on a level with others, for on it depended the answer to the question put earlier in this letter. 'Am I not an apostle? Have I not seen the Lord?' (9:1). Since he had already told the Galatians that the revelation to him had been *in* him, the third of the accounts of the appearances on the road to Damascus seems to be right in calling it a 'heavenly vision' involving a light he had seen, and a voice he had heard, presumably 'in' his brain (Acts 26:12–18). The other accounts say that his companions 'heard the voice but saw no one' (9:7) or 'saw the light but did not hear the voice' (22:8), presumably again without seeing Christ – which suggests that 'Luke' could not reproduce an accurate report and was not greatly troubled. What he does make clear is that he was sure that 'a young man named Saul' who was present did not share the dying Stephen's vision of 'the heavens opened and the Son of Man standing' (Acts 7:54–60).

It has been claimed that the body of the risen Jesus had to be in some way physical in order to assure Christians of the glory awaiting them in their own resurrections. But Paul taught in this letter to Corinth that while the dead will have a body (*soma*) it will not be one of flesh (*sarx*): it will be imperishable because immortal. A mortal body is like a seed to which God gives vitality (*psyche*) because he gives it some of his own spirit (*pneuma*), but it is different from 'the body of glory' since 'flesh and blood cannot inherit the kingdom of God' (15:36–56). Accordingly, Christ who has been 'raised from the dead, the first fruits of those who have died' (15:20), has become a 'life-giving spirit' as the 'man of heaven', and we shall be like him when 'all will be made alive in Christ . . . so that God may be all in all' (15:22, 28). In his second letter to Corinth he further explained his faith (4:16—5:5). It was that there will be 'a building from God, not made with hands, eternal in the heavens'. With that we shall be 'clothed' so that 'what is mortal may be swallowed up by life', 'by an eternal weight of glory beyond all measure'. And in that faith Paul did not 'lose heart' as he faced his share of the difficulties of life before admission to 'what cannot be seen' because it is 'eternal'.

His life was based on what he had experienced and out of the mass of evidence that this was the truth about him, we may pick a little of the proof that Paul became a new man in the down-to-earth sense that his personality was changed.

His letters display a man always intensely proud of being a Jew and always a rabbi well equipped and able to argue about the significance of the Bible of the Jews. He told the Philippians (3:4–6) that before his conversion he had been a Pharisee who was blameless according to the religious law and so full of zeal that he had 'persecuted the Church'. He sounds like the boastful Pharisee pinned down by Jesus in the parable. In Acts he is repeatedly shown as proud to be a Roman citizen: he confined his missionary work to the Roman empire; unlike Jesus he was eloquent in defending himself before imperial officials, and he exercised his legal right to 'appeal to Caesar' over all their heads. His letters show that he never condemned the vast institution of slavery on which the entire economy of the empire depended, that he thought that men who would not work should be left to starve (2 Thessalonians 3:10), and that he reckoned women to be reflections of men and not of God (2 Corinthians 11:5). He was no rebel.

And he was not a team player. In Acts, John Mark leaves him during a missionary journey, and when Barnabas wants to give the young man another chance they have a violent quarrel and part company, although previously Barnabas had been his (much needed) sponsor and senior. He seems to have been happier when working on his own, more or less under the authority of the church in Antioch, and to have been more fulfilled when after another quarrel, with Peter and Barnabas in Antioch, he worked as an independent missionary. He had an uneasy relationship with the church in Jerusalem, mainly as a fund-raiser at a distance, and he told the Galatians that any orders from its 'acknowledged leaders' made 'no difference to me'. In the controversy about circumcision they could go and 'castrate themselves' for all that he cared (2:7, 5:12). His letters show that he dominated the churches he founded, requiring love as well as obedience and pleading for respect or sympathy as he poured out his heart, getting at least near to self-pity. It became his policy not to begin any work in places where there were already Christians (Romans 15:20), and when he made an exception because he wanted to pause in Rome on his way to Spain, he prepared the ground by the longest and greatest of his letters, setting out the teaching he gave on his own authority as 'an apostle set apart for the gospel of God'.

But even as he made that claim his proudest boast to the Romans was to be 'a slave of Jesus Christ' (1:1). In his first letter to Corinthians he said that Christ had changed the ultimate meaning of everything: now he knew that 'through' him 'are all things' and 'through' him 'we exist' (8:6). More clearly, he had learned that the 'grace' of Christ was strong enough to see him through any new trial or old temptation. To be an adult is to be 'patient, kind, not envious or boastful or arrogant or rude' (1 Corinthians 13). At the end of his letter to the Galatians he wrote in large letters: 'May I never boast of anything except the cross of our Lord Jesus Christ by which the world has been crucified to me and I to the world.' Like a tough soldier he was more proud of his scars than of any decoration: 'I carry the marks of Jesus branded on my body.'

While a prisoner he told the Philippians that 'Christ Jesus has made me his own', his captive. He had more reasons for self-confidence than anyone else, having been a blameless and zealous Jew, but for Christ's sake he had lost everything and now he counted it all as rubbish: 'I want to know Christ and the power of his resurrection and the sharing of his sufferings by becoming like him in his death' (3:10). And death was to come to him through execution, probably in AD 64 under the emperor Nero, whom he had once called a 'servant of God' bearing the sword of justice (Romans 13:4).

Some of the most impressive passages in the New Testament come in the first of three letters of a teacher calling himself only 'the elder' or 'the presbyter': 'God is light and in him there is no darkness at all . . . God is love and those who abide in love abide in God, and God abides in them . . . Since God loved us so much, we also ought to love one another . . . We know that we have passed from death to life because we love one another . . . There is no fear in love . . . This is the victory that conquers the world, our faith'. But a closer inspection shows that the community addressed has the recognisable characteristic of a sect. Anyone who does not believe as this group is instructed to believe 'does not have God' and is not to be admitted to a true believer's house (2 John 9, 10). In contrast, no one who does so believe is capable of sin (1 John 3:6).

In the gospel associated with this community it is not clear that any direct use is made of the other gospels, although they have in common some traditions about Jesus in slightly different versions. Other historical material is used, it seems, but it may be said that nowadays this gospel would properly be classified as fiction, the facts in it being like the facts in an historical novel. To say that may seem brutal and forgetful of the way in which the gospel has fed, and still feeds, the spiritual lives of Christians (including me). But a novel of rare quality can be a far deeper commentary on the human situation in general than is possible for a precisely and exclusively factual study, and the point being made is that if we seek the truth about Jesus this gospel presents us with a 'truth' substantially different from the truth found in the other gospels and it becomes our duty to look closely.

The other gospels are closer to the historical facts, one being that Jesus almost never talked clearly about himself. The closest which this evidence gets to the claims in the fourth gospel is this: 'no one knows the Father or who the Father is, except the Son and anyone to whom the Son chooses to reveal him' (Matthew 11:25–27; Luke 10:21–22). But it is often thought that this claim loses much of its almost Johannine force if the capital letters are removed from the English and if it is remembered that this is in a prayer addressed devoutly to 'Abba, Lord of heaven and earth'. In the fourth gospel we find quite long speeches about himself addressed by Jesus to Jews with very little explanation of his claims to be the true temple (2:21), the Messiah (as early as 4:26), the bread which gives life to the world (6:33–36), and eternal life (6:47), the light of the world (8:12) but himself 'not of this world' (8:23), with threats such as 'you will die in your sins unless you believe that I am . . . the Son of Man' (8:24, 28). Instead of the emphasis on healings as signs of the arrival of the kingdom of God, there are 'signs' which reveal the glory of Jesus. More than a hundred gallons of water are turned into wine for a wedding (2:1–11) and his last miracle before his own resurrection is the raising of Lazarus who has been four days in the tomb. This is said to be the reason why the Jewish authorities sought his death (11:1–53), since the cleansing of the temple has been presented as the start, not the climax, of the mission (2:13–22). Instead of the many human touches in the other gospels including parables using everyday life, we have sayings which are both demanding and enigmatic. Instead of our meeting a man who can be uncertain, afraid and exhausted, this Jesus knows beforehand everything that is to 'happen' to him and remains in control of every situation until his work has been accomplished triumphantly (18:4, 19:25–30). As early as 4:42 he has been hailed by Samaritans as 'the Saviour of the world' and as early as 1:29 John the Baptist has declared that he 'takes away the sin of the world'.

The speeches in this gospel have been misunderstood when regarded as the teaching of the historical Jesus: they resemble the letters from the risen Jesus to the seven churches of Asia in the Revelation of John (a different author). When read as arising from the profound devotion of the Johannine community, and from its feeling of isolation from a world which hates them (15:19), their motivation is easily respected. Nevertheless, they present a Jesus who is scarcely human despite his 'flesh'. It is claimed that 'the Father . . . has given all judgement to the Son', that 'unless you eat the flesh of the Son of Man and drink his blood you have no life in you', that 'before Abraham was I am' (5:22, 6:53, 8:58). Jesus rebukes 'the Jews' who believe that 'we have one father, God himself' with this retort: 'You are from your father the devil' (8:41, 44). And the Jesus of this gospel is also different from the Jesus of history in that he does not work mainly among the poor and in Galilee. 'Jesus began to weep' (11:35) is a rare glimpse of a man to be loved.

Some evidence has survived that 'the presbyter' who wrote this gospel and the letters was called John and the community he led is nowadays called Johannine. There is, however, a complication: 'we', presumably members of the community, added to the gospel at 21:24 a claim that it had been written by an unnamed disciple 'whom Jesus loved' and who had 'reclined next to Jesus at the supper' (as in 13:23–25). But none of the other gospels mentions this disciple and even here no explanation is offered as to how he became the favourite. Late in the second century he was thought to be John, one of the two sons of Zebedee who are mentioned in Mark's gospel as young fishermen, nicknamed the Sons of Thunder and rebuked for wanting to sit next to Jesus in glory (1:19, 3:17, 10:35) – scarcely ideal circumstances in which to be uniquely intimate in a spiritual communion. In this gospel these brothers are mentioned only at 21:2. It has therefore been thought possible that the beloved disciple never existed in history but was an ideal figure personifying the devotion of the Johannine community. In his first letter 'the presbyter' claims that 'we have seen with our eyes' and 'touched with our hands' the 'word' of 'the eternal life that was with the Father' (1:1, 2), but this claim can be defended only if it means that humans could see and touch Jesus. The beloved disciple may have existed but the gospel cannot be based on the memory in about AD 95 of someone who in AD 30 was an adult able to persuade a suspicious doorkeeper to admit Peter (18:15–17) and to take the bereaved mother of Jesus into his own home (19:26, 27). If he did found the Johannine community and teach it, any historical information which he shared was, it seems, dwarfed by spiritual insights which the community including the author of this gospel and the letters developed.

What this author really believed about the resurrection of Jesus is not entirely clear, because he imagines the spiritual life which is his main concern in a style which can be called materialistic. In the teaching which he attributes to Jesus are adjacent sentences (5:24–29). The spiritual: 'Very truly I tell you, anyone who hears my word and believes him who sent me has eternal life, and does not come under judgement, but has passed from death to life.' The material: 'Very truly I tell you, the hour is coming, and is now here, when the dead will hear the voice of the Son of God' . . . when all who are in their graves will come out –

those who have done good, to the resurrection of life, and those who have done evil, to the resurrection of condemnation.'

But it may well be thought that if we seek to know what spiritual experience is reflected in this extraordinary gospel, we do best to listen to this gospel's account of the last supper of Jesus and his disciples. There the Lord washes the world's dirt from the disciples' feet while knowing that 'he had come from God and was going to God', having 'conquered the world'. He makes them 'entirely clean' because they now 'share' in his life. He gives them peace of mind, for he is united with them as branches are with a vine: they live in him, he lives in them. The 'Spirit of truth' sent by him (but coming from the Father) reminds them of what he taught when with them physically but also declares what is 'true' although not taught then. In their Spirit-filled community the old commandment to love the neighbour has been made new: 'love one another just as I have loved you.' Knowing that love, they are filled with a gladness not known to the world because it is a part of his eternal joy. They are already eternal, because to be eternal is to know 'the one true God and Jesus Christ' sent by him (as is said at 17:3 in the middle of a prayer ascribed to Jesus). This is life in the light of Easter.

When this light dawns in this gospel, we see the same combination of the material and the spiritual, with the spirit prevailing since 'what is born of the Spirit is spirit' (3:6). When Mary of Magdala finds that 'the stone had been removed from the tomb' this merely makes her weep, but the disciple whom Jesus loved beats Peter in a race to the tomb and 'believes' when he deduces from the corpse's abandoned wrappings that it has dematerialised. Mary is so blinded by her tears that she thinks that the figure in the garden is the gardener, and when she knows better she is told not to hold on to him, 'because I have not yet ascended to the Father' (20:1–18): fuller seeing and touching will be possible then. But she, not Peter, is the first to see the risen Jesus, presumably because a woman is more spiritual than a man.

That evening Jesus appears despite locked doors and the fears still in the hearts of the disciples whom he has already called 'my brothers'. We are to think of him as already 'ascended', already in eternity and already able to 'send' the Holy Spirit, although in the Acts of the Apostles many days must pass before the final ascension and the gift of the Spirit. Jesus brings peace and the power to forgive themselves and others; that they are themselves forgiven is gently implied. For the Johannine community this does not refer to the absolution of sins by a priest in private, a practice which was not known before the seventh century and was suspect when it was introduced from Ireland; it was made compulsory before the Easter communion in the Western Church only in 1215. Early on, sinners had been excommunicated until they had served public humiliation and severe penance among the penitents, before their readmission by the bishop. (The beginnings of this practice lie behind 2 Corinthians 2:5–11.) For the Johannine community it was clear that forgiveness came direct from God through Jesus and that any Christian acting as a deputy of Jesus could pray for someone else to be forgiven provided that the sin was not so serious as to deserve eternal death (1 John 5:16). So it seems that in the Johannine gospel the power to release from sin is given to the whole community, together with the power to say who is, and who is not, forgivable.

A week later Jesus appears again, to assure Thomas who had been absent and who had not believed the report of the other disciples. The body of Jesus is so definitely physical that it is marked by the scars left by the nails and the spear, but instead of accepting the invitation to test this physicality, Thomas immediately addresses Jesus as if he were a Roman emperor, 'Lord and God'. Behind the telling of this story there may be a dialogue between the Johannine community and the community which was behind the non-biblical Gospel of Thomas, where the whole emphasis is on 'spirit' as contrasted with the 'flesh' in which the Jesus of John 'came' and was 'seen'. But the communities of John and Thomas could have agreed on the climax to this story: 'Blessed are those who have not seen and yet have come to believe.'

Another appearance by the risen Jesus is related in chapter 21, added after the gospel's conclusion, probably by another author. The authority of 'the disciple whom Jesus loved' is claimed for its story by the use of 'we', but the action in this epilogue is more physical than in the first three appearances. Jesus is seen on the shore when seven disciples including Thomas have resumed work as fishermen. As daylight comes Jesus tells them where fish are to be found, cooks breakfast and forgives Peter three times for having denied knowing him three times. Peter is reduced to the basic Christian response in extreme simplicity: 'You know that I love you.' Then he is told not to be curious about the future of 'the disciple whom Jesus loved'; the rumour that Jesus promised that the disciple would never die is denied in a comment. Finally the command 'Follow me!' given on this beach in Galilee envisages Peter's crucifixion in Rome.

This epilogue may reflect a new agreement between the followers of Peter and the Johannine community, drawn together by the risen and eternal Lord. Certainly it reflects, with imperishable beauty, the Christian experience of being confronted both by the claims of Christ and by his forgiveness of failure. Here the presence of Christ is found both within the world of routine work and in the costly mission to the unbelieving world. But questions can be asked even while the spiritual power of these stories about 'signs' is revered. How could the risen Jesus speak to Mary, yet still be thought to be a gardener? How would Mary hinder his 'ascent to the Father' if she held on to his body? Had he not already been exalted to Paradise? How was the body then made physical – indeed, wounded – before people in a locked room? How were the materials for breakfast obtained? If Peter had been among the disciples at the earlier appearances, why does this encounter sound like the first since his denials? But such questions would not touch the purpose of these 'signs' of the resurrection. In the vegetable garden outside the tomb is death-defying love. In the defensively locked room is eternal forgiveness. On the beach in Galilee is a new dawn in the world's dark and futile history.

Inevitably this new age, called by Jesus the kingdom of God, has been pictured in terms of a physical transformation of the world, believed to be necessary if the real world is ever to be brought under the rule of the One pictured as the King. Also inevitably, the people of this new age, raised above death, have been pictured with glorified bodies more or less like their mortal bodies, preserving their personal identities. And it has been taught for many centuries, and believed by many millions, that this new age was inaugurated by the raising of the Lord's own body so that it could be made articulate, mobile and able to appear and disappear at will, but also clothed normally and able to eat or cook, as a foretaste of the destiny of the universe and of humankind.

However, it does not seem probable that Jesus expected a physical resurrection either for himself in the immediate future or for anyone in 'the age to come'. The gospels include predictions such as 'after three days rise again' (Mark 8:31), but these seem to have been added to Christian traditions after the event, for all the gospels except John's clearly suggest that Jesus did not go to his death confident that it would be reversed so quickly and so dramatically, nor do they suggest that his disciples went to his tomb thinking that this was a possibility. And these gospels do report that when he was questioned about the general idea of 'resurrection' shortly before his death, Jesus did not offer one of the hopes for the glorious reconstruction of the physical world which seem to have been common in his time. Instead, he taught that when 'people rise from the dead, they are like angels in heaven.' They will not lose their identities, however, for God will love and sustain them one by one: he has been and is 'the God of Abraham, the God of Isaac and the God of Jacob' (Mark 12:18–27). In Luke's gospel the dead will 'live to' God, their life being directly and completely dependent on his (20:27–40). In keeping with this denial that a physical resurrection will be needed, 'Luke' says that when their deaths were imminent Jesus assured the criminal next to him, 'Truly I tell you, today you will be with me in Paradise' (23:43). There is no hint that here 'Paradise' means anything less than heaven: in the parable, Lazarus does not have to wait for a physical resurrection in order to enjoy life in the Paradise to which angels have taken him (16:23–26). Inevitably 'Luke' imagines heaven, and resurrection into it, in physical images and it is relevant that the word 'Paradise' came from the Persian for 'garden'. But the teaching of Jesus himself is presented as being simple and clear: people in eternity do not marry because they are no longer physical.

That does not mean that they are no longer real. Jesus and Christians over many centuries would not call 'angels' unreal; the word comes from the Greek for 'messengers', and these have been believed in as mysterious envoys from God. They have also been pictured as having their own special bodies including wings for flight through the air, and therefore in modern times they have often been left to adorn the realm of art, but in the old days they had a far stronger status in religion. Similarly, a 'vision' can have great power in the history of religion although the word 'illusion' may follow rapidly in much modern thought. But the Oxford English Dictionary gives a meaning for 'vision' which modern Christians may use in the present connection: 'an appearance of a prophetic or mystical character, or having the nature of a revelation, supernaturally presented to the mind in sleep or in an abnormal state'. An 'appearance' of that kind need not depend on the action of seeing with the bodily eye, but it can depend on action by the eternal God, sending signals from outside to the human brain. In our time it could be said to be a phone call or e-mail from heaven.

Of course any such vision must use material already accumulated in memories of earlier experiences, and it is also obvious that the brain can often use such material to construct pictures which are imagined without any input from reality. Also it must be agreed that a human element is at work when pictures and words are used in order to report the vision to others. A report can be comparatively straightforward, as when Paul says in his second letter to Corinth that after a time of intense prayer in distress he 'heard' the words 'My grace is sufficient for you, for power is made perfect in weakness' (12:8, 9). Or there can be an inability or refusal to report anything, as when Paul felt 'caught up into Paradise' and heard words so mysterious and sacred that 'they are not to be told' (12:1–47). But there can also be minor differences in stories, either when the originator tells them more than once or when they are passed on. Words 'heard' by Paul on the road to Damascus differ in different places in Acts (9:5, 22:8–10, 26:14–18). All this must be granted in any advocacy of visions as the facts behind the 'appearances' of the risen Lord, but that should not end our enquiry.

It is often said that mere visions could not account for the impact of that resurrection, for they would have been private not public, subjective not objective, at best arising from the subconscious depths of the believer's brain. And the Bible itself is full of warnings that dreams by night or visions by day may be misleading. But the Bible is also full of visions which it applauds, and a saying in Q (Matthew 7:16) supplies a down-to-earth test to be applied: 'You will know them by their fruits. Are grapes gathered from thorns, or figs from thistles?' In this case the fruit of a vision may be the life and work of St Paul, a reality on public view, or the undeniable reality of the spiritual life of the Johannine community. The power of visions may also be glimpsed at the beginning of the last and strangest book in the Christian Bible. There Jesus 'speaks' with a sword hanging from his mouth, yet the imagery seems to reflect a genuine experience. A Christian prophet praying one Sunday in an isolated prison camp 'sees' the risen Christ and falls at his feet 'as though dead'. Then he rises to be eloquent about visions of the future which are entirely imaginary but which have set other people's imaginations and lives on fire over many centuries because they are the work of an inspired visionary.

Many later visions of Jesus have been reported in many periods, including two by friends of mine who as a long-term result became much loved bishops. As a Jewish boy who had never read the gospels, Hugh Montefiore 'saw' Jesus in Rugby School and was told to follow him. As a religiously confused young man, Stephen Verney 'saw' Jesus while in Galilee and was told not take his doubts so seriously. I myself have not had a vision but I think I have had glimpses.

Like their faithful successors in every generation the early Christians lived and died in the conviction that 'the Lord is risen indeed', and their faith is reflected in the famous stories associated with Christmas, which since the conversion of the midwinter festival in Christianity's fourth century has so developed that it has been enjoyed more widely than any other annual celebration in the world's history. But what in this connection is the 'truth in its beauty' praised in a hymn as one of the best responses to all the wonderful imagery, music and merry-making?

One truth is conveyed in that the stories have a thoroughly Jewish setting. The mother of Jesus is promised that 'the Lord God will give to him the throne of his ancestor David', and she rejoices that the powerful are being brought down from their thrones and the rich are being sent away empty (Luke 1:32, 46–55). This promise and joy would not have been related at a time when the Jewish nation had been conquered by Rome, and Jesus crucified as a prelude to this disaster, had it not been believed that somehow already the Crucified had been enthroned and the poor, or some of them, had been given a new hope. The original setting, exclusively Jewish, had been transcended – but not forgotten.

Another truth is that after his resurrection Jesus was known to be *Emmanuel*, 'God with us', and the tributes were coming both from the simple and from the clever. So these stories could include not only shepherds who needed the small wage paid for going on the night shift (Luke 2:8–20) but also 'wise men' learned in astronomy and willing to undertake a long and dangerous journey in order to bring gifts fit for a king and a priest (Matthew 2:1–12). The birth could be seen as extraordinary because the life had been, reaching the common people but outreaching the wisdom of the wise.

However, this story telling also presents a problem to many in the modern world. In the ancient world the normal preliminaries to a birth were of course understood but stories about the miraculous births of gods and heroes were popular. For the modernised it is now taken for granted that being human, however grandly, involves having a biological father and mother, a fact already in the mind of Matthew when he explains the existence of the brothers and sisters of Jesus by saying that after the arrival of the firstborn Joseph and Mary did have marital relations (1:25). It therefore seems that all that is necessary, even about the birth of Jesus, is to believe that the 'power of the Most High' did 'overshadow' a woman and a man, spiritually making them the parents of the Lord (Luke 1:35).

It is not easy to believe that the birth took place in Bethlehem if we know that despite Luke's story about why this had to be, no census of the entire empire was attempted before AD 74, and that when a local census was arranged no one was ever compelled to register in the birthplace, which would have frustrated the purpose of the census – taxation. The census (not universal but local and under Quirinius) to which Luke (2:12) refers took place not while Herod was king but in AD 6 when Judea was taken under direct rule from Rome. It seems more likely that Mary and Joseph never left Nazareth to register in Bethlehem, the village near Jerusalem from which King David had emerged as Israel's greatest hero. Matthew believed that Joseph occupied a 'house' there until he made his home in Nazareth (2:11, 23), but he also claimed that the comet 'stopped' to indicate which the house was (2:9). He began with a family tree showing descent from David, in modern reckoning over about a thousand years, and extended it to Abraham, but Luke's genealogy (3:23–37) took a different route, back to Adam. Matthew claimed that Herod, a Jewish king, first did not know of a popular belief that as heir of David the Messiah would come from Bethlehem, and then did not hesitate to order a massacre of boys in and around Bethlehem for which there is no other evidence (2:1–6, 16–18). John's gospel mentions the belief (7:40–44) but instead of endorsing it gives us (like Mark) no story of a miracle in Bethlehem. Paul accepted the descent of Jesus from David (Romans 1:3), and this could be said to be part of his gospel (2 Timothy 2:8), but no theological use of this belief survives, and again there is no mention of Bethlehem. And Mark (12:35–37), strangely followed by Matthew and Luke, recorded a tradition that Jesus thought that the Messiah must be David's Lord, not his son, despite the popular use of 'Son of David' (e.g. Mark 10:47) to mean 'Messiah', or of 'our ancestor David' (e.g. 11:10) to mean 'we Jews'.

The greatest obstacle to taking the Christmas stories literally is the strong tradition that the family of Jesus did not understand why he had to leave them and his family-supporting job. This tradition, which is recorded in Mark 3:31–35 and reappears in John 7:1–9, is almost certainly based on fact, because it is very hard to imagine that it was invented at a time when the family is known to have been prominent in the foundation of the Christian movement. But the reaction by those closest to Jesus for most of his life would have been very odd indeed if Mary had remembered the prophecies, miracles and gifts. However, there are reasons which even an historian ought to take seriously for believing one miracle in Nazareth. What can be known about the parents of Jesus is that his relationship with Joseph was such that he called God *Abba*, and with Mary was such that throughout his life, despite everything that he endured, he felt loved and secure in his relationship with Abba: he had learned the meaning of love in his home. These facts will be all the more impressive if we think that this human couple had no memory of a supernatural birth and no complete understanding of their extraordinary son: they gave him love as they had given him life.

We cannot know the origin of Luke's story (2:41–52) of Jesus in the temple at the age of twelve, a story in which his parents maintain pious customs but get cross when their son is temporarily disobedient. But since Joseph then disappears from the gospels, we may link him in our reflections with Luke's other story of old Simeon departing in peace, although Mary was to live and learn how a sword could pierce a soul (2:22–38).

Recent investigations have given a new weight to Mary's question in Luke's gospel, 'How can this be?' (1:34). It has been discovered that Nazareth was then a village with some four hundred inhabitants. Most houses were shacks with caves behind them for storage and sleeping in the heat. The 'synagogue' would be a small hall, roughly built of stone and mud and used for social purposes without a resident rabbi, but there young boys would receive an elementary education before joining their fathers at work, perhaps as labourers building the nearby town of Sepphoris. So far as we know, Jesus took over Joseph's small business when his father died but in this unromantic environment made not a single friend with whom he could share his deepest thoughts. So far as we know, unlike his brothers (1 Corinthians 9:5) and almost everyone around him, he did not marry, and no disciple of his came from this place where he spent most of his life. Luke (4:16–30) tells a graphic story about his return to Nazareth when 'all were filled with rage' and tried to kill him. They had been fascinated to hear 'Joseph's son' preaching in the hall where he had learned to read and write, and they may also have been surprised that he could read from a scroll in the Bible, for the unpointed Hebrew script of that period was not easy for a carpenter to read. But he had offended them by saying that the great prophets of the past had been happy to heal people who were not Jews. At least this story shows the kind of place that the early Christians thought had been the scene of the bulk of their Lord's life. It seems that until his thirtieth year (or so) he kept his thoughts to himself, yet it was during that time (more than a lifetime for many of his contemporaries) that he worked out at least some of the stories and sayings which were to constitute his teaching for the people and for posterity, since it is incredible that this wealth of material had no preparation. He did it alone.

After his rejection by the only place he knew well, he made his base in Capernaum, which was slightly more sophisticated (a frontier town with a small fishing industry), but even there most of the houses were made of mud, as were the streets. Yet the gospels show that the man from Nazareth had by now a mind unquestionably in the first class and more than equal to any questioner or critic. His speech could be terrifying or elegant. He seems to have been at ease in supper parties with prostitutes or at dinner with a Pharisee. His knowledge of the Hebrew Bible would be a bit less unusual, but his ability to reinterpret it selectively, originally and radically was astonishing. It could at least be said that after a silence lasting for centuries a great prophet had arisen. People who knew where he had spent most of his life could ask 'Where did this man get all this?' (Mark 6:2), or 'Can anything good come out of Nazareth?' (John 1:46). 'John' prefers to picture him in Jerusalem (2:13–3:21, 5:1–47, 7:10–10:42, 12:12–20:29). For Mark in Rome the gospel can begin with this miracle: 'Jesus came from Nazareth of Galilee' (1:9).

The story of his 'virgin birth' (more accurately 'virginal conception') has often been linked with his divinity but modern theologians are agreed that there is no necessary connection. In the ancient world someone could be thought divine in some sense after a normal birth and someone born normally could be born, or reborn, spiritually 'not of blood or of the will of the flesh or of the will of man, but of God', as John's gospel says about Christians while remaining silent about how Jesus 'became flesh' (1:12, 13). Nor do we need to believe that Jesus clearly claimed to be 'God', for as we have seen his claim was to be God's unique servant, son, messenger and agent. Paul always distinguished between 'God' and Jesus Christ the 'Son of God', and 'Lord', although it is richly suggestive that he put 'the grace of the Lord Jesus Christ' before 'the love of God' at the end of his second letter to Corinth. It was through the grace that he knew the love. Christ was God's 'image' and his face was where he saw the glory of God (4:4, 6). In his first letter to Corinth he wrote plainly that 'there is one God, the Father, from whom are all things and for whom we exist.' Less clearly he refers to 'one Lord, Jesus Christ, through whom are all things and through whom we exist', which teaches at least that Christ is the link between the Creator and the creation. In his letters to the Galatians (4:4) and to the Romans (8:3) he was content to say that 'God sent his Son.' What he wrote at Romans 9:5 was probably '. . . comes the Messiah. Over all, God is blessed for ever. Amen.' In what seems to be a hymn quoted to the Philippians (2:6–11) this uniqueness is expressed by saying that Jesus was 'in the form of God' and equal with God before he 'emptied himself' and 'took the form of a slave' by being born and by dying before 'God highly exalted him' and gave him 'the name that is above every name'. But now 'every knee should bow' at the name of Jesus, while still not identifying Jesus with God. But Paul's point may be that Jesus was humble, unlike Adam who was made 'in the image of God' but sinfully decided that he would be the one to tell the difference between good and evil (Genesis 1:27, 2:17).

In the letter to the Colossians, which may be from Timothy (named as the joint author), Christ is 'the image of the invisible God, the first-born of all creation'. In him and by him, through him and for him, all things were created and 'in him all the fullness of God was pleased to dwell'. But even here (1:15–20) 'God' and 'Christ' are two, as they are in the letters to Timothy. In the letter to the Hebrews (not rightly associated with Paul) 'Christ' is again in the first place after 'God'. He is 'the exact imprint of God's very being' but he is also definitely human: when young Jesus was yet to be made 'by the grace of God . . . perfect through sufferings' (2:9–10). In this letter he is the Christians' high priest in eternity, but he is not the One to whom the priest's sacrifice is offered.

That distinction between Jesus and God is reaffirmed in the letter to Titus (where 'our God and Saviour Christ Jesus' at 2:13 seems to be a mistake in some manuscripts). It is also found in all the gospels, even in John's when that is taken as a whole. Thomas calls the risen Jesus 'my Lord and my God' (20:28) but Jesus himself has just spoken of 'my Father and your Father, my God and your God' (20:17). 'I and my Father are one' (10:30) is followed by a claim to be no more than 'God's son' whom 'the Father has sanctified and sent into the world' (10:36). It seems possible to reconcile these statements by saying that the disciple finds God's presence and activity in Jesus uniquely because the relationship between the human Jesus and the divine One is unique.

In the prologue to John's gospel we read that 'the Word was with God and the Word was God' but any confusion is eased by the teaching that 'all things came into being' through the Word (*Logos*). By implication this identifies the Word with 'Wisdom' in the Hebrew Bible, where it is a personified because poetic way of referring to the wisdom of the Creator (Proverbs 8:22–31). Today we might speak more credibly by clearly avoiding the danger of that personification being misunderstood as a claim that billions of years before being born, Jesus created the universe in something of the style in which he was to make things in his carpenter's workshop. We could say that the Big Bang was not completely an accident, nor was the evolution of life on Earth, nor was the birth of Jesus: from the beginning the wise Creator had a plan eventually leading to that birth. We cannot fully understand this plan but we can glimpse it as the ultimate meaning of all history and as the light which has never been overcome. And we can rejoice that God's wisely creative plan was embodied in what we can understand: a human life with 'a glory as of a father's only son'. This man from Nazareth 'lived among us and we have seen his glory' (John 1:5, 14).

~

FIVE

YES TO HIM NOW

Jesus was a layman who wanted a religion for the laity. Without condemning practices such as frequent worship in church, prolonged contemplation of God and many loving intercessions, it may be observed as a fact that in his own teaching Jesus concentrated on private prayer which inspires the humble service of the Father in practical acts of love. He lived among people who had little privacy; in his small home of Nazareth, occupied by a large family and including a workshop, presumably most of his praying was done outdoors – as was his later practice, sometimes for a whole night (e.g. Luke 6:12–16). Matthew has him saying that where doors were available (how often were they?) they should be shut so that prayer could be secret, and that empty phrases should not be heaped up in worship (6:5–8).

Obviously it would be utterly wrong to abandon all the praise of God apart from the reference to Abba in the Lord's Prayer, but according to Jesus what Abba wants most is that he should be allowed to govern the world. So that is the right context in which the news of our world may be brought before our Creator who already knows and understands the world – and loves it – far more thoroughly than we do. He does not need to be informed or persuaded what to do. In the Lord's Prayer the prayer is that his name may be hallowed in the way he chooses, by the fulfilment of his purpose that his kingdom may come on earth – again, in the way he chooses. One great purpose of our thinking about the world in prayer is therefore to make us ask what God wants in a particular situation – including what God wants us to do, even if this means no more than involvement by voting, if we live in a democracy. It is inevitable that we should want prayer to change God's will as well as our actions, and those who make such prayers can tell of divine action for which they give thanks – but equally, people who pray in great anxiety or grief can feel after getting no result that God is deaf, because it seems that his will is to let nature or history take its course. The only clear instruction that emerges from the story of Jesus himself is that we should pray in light or darkness, and go on praying amid failures to get the response we want. His main command, delivered most movingly in the garden of Gethsemane, is not that we should understand God but that we should place ourselves at his service. And if we pray and resolve in this way which Jesus taught, we need to pray also, every day, for our food as fuel and our forgiveness as the only cure for what we still are.

The lifestyle of Jesus was very different from the lives of almost all of us who, while trying to follow, have had the opportunity to live more comfortably than he did, and perhaps all that we can say if we are honest is that we are challenged to self-denial by him and his saints. That is also the case if we claim to live 'according to the Sermon on the Mount' while being in fact bogged down in compromises. Our defence can be that our circumstances are different from a mission in Galilee long ago. To this plea Jesus would surely not be deaf (it is reported that in Jerusalem he allowed his disciples to carry daggers for self-defence), but we need a light we can see while we stumble in the muck. The Orthodox or Catholic tradition of the veneration of saints encourages us not to be excessive in compromises, although it is a pity that this glorious company has so far included almost no married adults with ordinary jobs.

A major example of difficulty in bridging gaps between times and cultures is the gulf between belief in the influence of invisible spirits and belief in a scientific diagnosis. Jesus lived, thought and worked in a pre-scientific time and culture, and there are still many places where the mental world of his followers is like that. But in societies based on the application of science Christians have to live, think and work in a world very different from the world of the Bible – and here is another challenge to use God-given brains.

In recent years a vital part of the kingdom of God has 'come' in the shape of improvements in health care or at least in the shape of concern for the millions who cannot afford to be healthy. And many branches of the Christian Church have responded by the revival of their own 'ministry of healing'. All this calls for celebration, but here again the style of Jesus presents a challenge. It is becoming increasingly clear that professional medicine must continue to use, and improve, the pill and the knife, yet within the unavoidable limits of time and resources the aim must be more person-to-person healing, with the expert respond-ing to the whole person – while professional religion must not degener-ate into instant, dramatic and well-publicised 'miracle cures' for applause. And perhaps the biggest challenge is to the average Christian congregation. In the light of the practice of Jesus as healer, it can be seen that the long fight of every church must be against everything that damages the health of divinely created bodies – a fight in which

Christians must be models in the renunciation of demonic habits as a better lifestyle is chosen for God's sake, for the sake of the Creator of this marvel, the body. Many patterns of church life are questioned by the fact that very large numbers now look elsewhere – to traditional medicine in strongly traditional societies, or to non-scientific healing when societies are modern or postmodern – in the belief that were they to turn to the Church of Jesus they would be asked about their health politely but not helped to be healthy.

When Jesus demonstrated in the temple that in particular he had been sent to heal the sickness of hatred between Jew and Gentile, he dramatically inaugurated Christianity as an international religion. It was to be almost identified with the Byzantine empire, with the Christendom of western Europe, with the nationalism of the Protestant Reformation, with the Spanish, Portuguese, Dutch, British and French empires, and with the expansive confidence of Europe as its twentieth century began and of the USA as it ended – but always what Jesus did in the Court of the Gentiles was on record, and universality revived when empires and nations lost power as they always do. In our own time the global Yes to Jesus is being articulated in images of him in many colours and clothes and with many titles. No other religion – not even Islam – has generated an international life at this depth and breadth because no other religion has been so quick to break down the separating walls of nationality, race, language and culture to make 'a great multitude that no one could number' (Revelation 7:9). It was the soaring vision of Paul that 'there is no longer Jew or Greek, there is no longer slave or free, there is no longer male and female: for all of you are one in Christ Jesus' (Galatians 3:28). And this vision has now to be turned into ever-increasing reality, with an unprecedented opportunity on a global scale. To walk into any church ought to mean walking into the world.

The whole elaborate apparatus of ancient Israel's national shrine was replaced for Christians when the last supper was held obscurely a short distance from it. The Letter to the Hebrews does not pause to clarify whether or not the temple is still standing, but the anonymous author's thrust is to celebrate its replacement by Christ as the true 'high priest' offering himself as a sacrifice acceptable to God, within a new agreement between God and humankind which makes possible a new way of living in a new faith. Rightly the Eucharist ('Thanksgiving') has been at the heart of the international Church's worship throughout its history, and despite many disagreements about its precise significance, new agreements were reached in the twentieth century.

It ought to be presided over by an authorised servant and

representative of Christ but it should involve everyone present. It remembers the death but also the birth, life and resurrection, and although it does not repeat any past event the drama can make the past live for the worshippers. The bread and wine are not changed physically but (somewhat as in modern currency a piece of paper may be worth a sum of money) the one now signifies Christ's body and therefore his person, and the other means his life and therefore his self-sacrifice. In the years to come many new forms of communication will be used by Christians as they have been in the past, and these may not always involve face-to-face meetings, for the electronic revolution has begun. New methods including TV, videos and the internet are vital if the good news is to reach people who would be mystified or scandalised if apparently asked to eat human flesh and drink human blood, and not interested if asked to sing songs of praise themselves. But nothing will replace the face-to-face assembly of a mixed community to share bread and wine, remembering the self-sacrifice which did result in dead flesh and dried blood. To do that we must meet. And as those who plan and lead worship are encouraged to be imaginative, other means may be developed to reach the people in the style of Jesus.

And it seems that the Lord who did not hesitate to eat and drink with tax collectors and prostitutes, as well as with Pharisees, would not wish us to be too choosy about the fellow humans with whom we are willing to share Holy Communion. At the last supper the guests of Jesus were disciples who were soon to 'become deserters' (Matthew 26:31). Before that they had gone to sleep in Gethsemane, and before that they had argued about 'which one of them was to be regarded as the greatest' (Luke 21:24–27). In John's gospel (13:26–30) only one disciple is mentioned as being given bread by Jesus – but he is Judas Iscariot.

If encouraging agreements have been reached about the Eucharist, that has not yet become true about the self-sacrifice which it re-presents. Among all the interpretations taught in earlier ages, the strongest survivor in the modern period is the doctrine that since the beginning of the human ability to misuse free will – in biblical terms, since the Fall of Adam and Eve – humankind has been so full of sin that God has been full of wrath and his justice has had to be satisfied. It is believed that this has been possible only because Christ accepted the punishment due for all the sins of the world, so that God can now forgive us for Christ's sake – and that is still for many millions the heart of the good news. But many modern Christians have rejected this theory of the atonement, partly because they do not find it set forth clearly in the Bible.

The Revelation of John (5:6) has made the image of Jesus as the innocent lamb slaughtered in sacrifice but now standing in heaven important for Christian devotion. But it is now generally agreed by scholars that the Jewish sacrificial system which is the background to this image did not have as its main idea to 'propitiate', appease or placate an angry God. Instead, the emphasis was on the need to remove any destructive sense of being guilty and unclean which might remain after receiving God's forgiveness of the repentant sinner. Because this was the emphasis, Judaism survived, and even became more intensely devout, when the temple had been destroyed and Jews had been forbidden to enter the pagan city which had replaced their Jerusalem. When in modern times Jews began to return to their ancient land in large numbers, the reconstruction of the temple was scarcely mentioned in the agenda of the Zionist movement and is today advocated by only a small minority. Even when the temple was the centre for devotion, provision was made for the symbolic heaping of Israel's sins on the head of a goat driven into the wilderness (Leviticus 16:1–22). 'The lamb of God who takes away the sins of the world' (John 1:29) refers to this. And even when sacrifices were valued highly, Psalm 50, sung or recited in the temple, declared plainly that God is not interested in any sacrifice unless it is preceded by repentance, social justice and self-discipline. Psalm 51 is a famous example of a penitent's call to God for mercy. It offers the sacrifice of 'a broken and contrite heart': after but not before this, God will give a 'clean heart' and will accept a sacrifice. Great prophets could be misunderstood as attacking the entire sacrificial system because their denunciations of any idea that forgiveness could be purchased by a sacrifice were so frequent and so fiercely eloquent.

However, Leviticus is a manual of practical instructions, not a theological treatise, and it would be natural for some people to think that they were paying for forgiveness, as when in a modern society a bunch of flowers bought in a shop is offered as a substitute for a more painful apology. The sacrificial system could be misunderstood as teaching that 'without the shedding of blood there is no forgiveness of sins' (Hebrews 4:22). It is at least possible that priests who lived off the system encouraged this unbiblical idea. But Paul did not teach that Christ's blood had to be shed in order to purchase forgiveness. He called for repentance as eloquently as any of the prophets or psalmists, but for him God's righteousness is shown when he 'passes over' sins without inflicting the punishment which everyone deserves because 'all have sinned' (Romans 3:21–26). The way in which Paul imagines the punishment of the impenitent draws on the Hebrew Scriptures, as do the warnings by Jesus in the gospels: those who choose to 'obey wickedness' must expect 'anguish and distress' after 'wrath and fury'. That pictures the infinitely sad disappointment of God and the infinitely stupid misery of sinners who, however, to the end refuse to repent. Yet these do not end in indefinitely prolonged pain: they 'perish' (2:1–12). And Paul concentrates on the future of sinners who respond with the faith or trust which gives their loving father access to them. Immediately he treats them as if they were already righteous; he 'justifies' them, seeing in them the potential which Christ revealed (4:1–5, 11). And then they are made righteous by, so to speak, dying and rising with Christ: they accept any cost in order to win that prize (6:1–11). It can be said that Christ is now 'in' them, or that the Spirit leads them, or that the Spirit gives them the power to cry 'Abba! Father!' (8:1–18). And the glory into which they enter is infinitely greater than 'the sufferings of this present time', because it is the glory revealed by the Christ 'who died, yes, was raised' – the glory of God's love (8:19–39). This glory is intended by God to be shared with all: the 'full number' of the peoples of the world will 'come in' and 'all Israel will be saved', for 'God has imprisoned all in disobedience so that he may have mercy on all' (11:25–36). That conclusion still astonishes Paul.

In Romans 3:25 the Greek word *hilasterion* was translated as 'propitiation' (an echo from the Latin) in the old English versions but the New Revised Standard Version (for example) has simply 'sacrifice of atonement' and that is also the case when the word comes in the first letter of John (2:2, 4:10). In the long discourse at the last supper in John's gospel no mention is made of the Son's need to propitiate the Father, and that is true of the other gospels and of Luke's reconstruction of what Peter preached when full of the Holy Spirit, although it is already being said that the crucifixion was 'according to the definite plan and foreknowledge of God' (Acts 1:23). It does not seem that Christians should now feel compelled to use an explanation of the at-one-ment which can suggest that the heavenly Father demands penal suffering before he is willing to forgive his children. No decent human parent would behave like that, so why should God? Indeed, how could God? Nor can it be necessary to compare the divine Judge with a human judge who might demand that an innocent man should be tortured to death while the obviously guilty culprit walks free. In any decent human system of justice, such a judge would be lucky to escape prison by pleading a mental illness which would prevent a fair trial.

So is a more credible interpretation of the cross available?

The best image seems to be of the crucifixion as martyrdom – of Jesus and his Father. The idea of martyrdom is not strange to any culture in the world; death is honoured as the price paid for the defence or the liberation of a nation or of an oppressed group within a nation, or for the success of some other good cause. Paul also taught that 'God sent his son to redeem', to pay the price needed if the children of God were to be more than slaves to evil (Galatians 4:4, 5). But he never added that the price is payable to God, and in common talk about a martyr's death it is never said to be demanded by anything other than an evil situation. There need be no thought that if Jesus interpreted his death as a 'ransom' he had in mind anything other than its costliness, which for him would mean death. In history, including recent years, a martyr's courage has often accepted death. Then that death may so have moved large numbers of people that the martyr's cause has made progress and even triumphed, for there is an instinctive agreement that 'no one has greater love than this, to lay down one's life for one's friends' (John 15:13).

The interpretation of Christ's death as a ransom meant much to Christians in an age when many of them were either slaves entirely at the mercy of their owners, or else 'free' people who were not free from poverty or from foreign control. In the Revelation of John the vision of Christ as a slaughtered lamb before the throne of God was understood as a ransom (5:6–14). But in later times, as Christian theology was taught by bishops, it was asked to whom the ransom was paid and the answer became 'the Devil', before it was asked why the Devil had been given any right to receive it. When people were told that the Devil had not been able to keep it, since Jesus had been raised from death, it was also asked why God had stooped to trickery. So Archbishop Anselm proposed a theory which reflected the social system of the Middle Ages: if a tenant failed to produce what a landowner or a king had a right to demand, compensation had to be paid.

Then a philosopher who was not a bishop but a celebrated lover, Peter Abelard, raised theology to a new level by teaching that the cross displays such love in the Son, and in the Father, that it arouses our love, repentance and desire to live a life of holy love. Yet his interpretation was seen to be inadequate because it failed to take account of the full gravity and strength of human sin, needing for its cure 'salvation', something more than a good example. The medieval Church therefore developed an elaborate system in which penitents were absolved after private confessions to priests who instructed them to express their repentance by acts of piety and by good works, which could include financial contributions. The Church had this power to absolve sinners because the 'merit' of the Son's death had been so great that it was more than any just payment to the Father, and the surplus had been shared with the Church as a treasury from which individual pardons could be drawn. The payment of the Son's human life had been necessary in order to 'propitiate' God – a doctrine made obligatory for Catholics after a decree of the Council of Trent in 1563.

The Protestant Reformers accepted this belief that the Father needed to be reconciled to us, but Martin Luther rejected most of the rest of the medieval system as a result of his experience in a monastery. A passionate man, he found that a pattern of frequent sins and confessions brought him no peace, as the strict observance of the Jewish religious law had brought no peace to Paul. Gradually he found in Paul a teacher of 'justification' by faith alone: if we have faith, meaning trust, in Christ's self-sacrifice, the amazing 'righteousness of God' means not that we are condemned but that we are treated as righteous before we actually are.

A partially different doctrine was taught by the other giant of sixteenth-century Protestantism, Jean Calvin. His mind was calmer, more organised and more legal. Wanting a new clarity, he simplified the explanation of the at-one-ment: Christ had paid the debt due to the Father. Puzzled as to why the discipline he demanded was not accepted by everyone in Geneva, he drew from some questioning passages in Paul's letter to Rome (9:1–29), and from Paul's great but selective interpreter Augustine, the belief that Christ died for the benefit only of those predestined or 'elected' by God to be saved, who might be few.

In modern times, however, most Protestants as well as Orthodox and Catholics have thought it incredible that God should predestine anyone to hell, and even Calvin thought the idea 'horrible'. They have also rejected Luther's insistence on a strongly emotional crisis of faith. They have preferred Paul's conclusion that so far from needing to be reconciled to us, it has always been God's intention to be merciful to all. Further, they have shared the belief that by his 'glory and goodness' Christ calls humans to be 'participants in the divine nature' (2 Peter 1:3–4). This *theosis* has always been the hope held out in the Orthodox Churches and despite the astounding wonder of this destiny it seems right for modern sinners who are prepared to have their lives changed after death, or preferably before it.

Evidently the New Testament does not offer a single, complete explanation of how Christ's death affects the at-one-ment in the new covenant between God and humankind. Nor has any doctrine about it been adopted as the teaching of the whole Church. In modern times these facts have given many Christians permission to think again, and an even stronger incentive has come from a deepened sensitivity to the evil in a world believed to have been made by the good God.

The terrible reality of evil in humans was made undeniable in the twentieth century by the wars and by the cold cruelty of Nazis and Communists, but this was also a time when it was seen more clearly than ever before how much pain and loss are parts of the workings of nature. All this made it impossible for most thinking people to believe either that God controls every event for a good purpose or that he will always intervene to put things right if asked. Christians have shared this profound questioning, but have found that the grim symbol of their faith, the cross, sheds a strange light, for it can be believed that in the crucified Christ is the suffering God. All his living creatures need to sacrifice themselves for the sake of others, and we may dare to say: so does he. But while creatures need to die in order to provide food or room for others, God must suffer simply because he loves his creatures who have to experience the pains which are within his creation.

Of course it must be added that if God suffers, and when 'in Christ' God goes through the experience of dying in acute pain, it must be in a divine way which we cannot fully understand, but that way may mean suffering more intense than anything known by any creature. Even so, the belief is bold and new. For many centuries Christian theology accepted the idea of God in much Greek philosophy, where the Unmoved Mover is incapable of suffering and of any other imperfection or change. Although in devotion 'God' could be on the cross, in theology it was taught that Christ's own suffering was not in his divine nature. But the modern belief can be connected with the Hebrew Bible, where God is affected by emotions shared with humans – by delight, anxiety, indignation, merciful kindness and sorrow, and by 'compassion', which implies some involvement in the suffering. He is affected by his creation, and in particular by the conduct of the people he has chosen to be his special agents. The God of Israel is never aloof. And when the Father of Jesus gives us a hard life, he invites us to share his suffering in a world where that is unavoidable. This is more than being sympathetic with us – and even more than being sympathetic with the suffering of his 'son' whom he has 'sent' while himself remaining at a distance. When we feel the pain, or enter the valley of the shadow of death, somehow so does God. There is nothing in anyone's suffering which does not correspond with what the whole of God knows from the inside. The God who may seem to have forsaken us is therefore our God, our God, and after that prayer on the cross there is no situation in which prayer to him cannot be made.

If 'Christ crucified' is proclaimed as 'the power of God and the wisdom of God' (1 Corinthians 1:23–25), inevitably it is foolishness to those in any generation who claim to be so wise that they know how illogical it is to think that the Source of all that exists has feelings at all like our own. It is also a scandal to orthodox Jews, Muslims and other devout believers in God, although they accept the possibility of some strong emotions such as wrath or pity in the Creator: they cannot think of God being a weak victim. But Christians need not regret that they are now criticised for this development of their constant belief that love is God's chief characteristic, for that criticism is better than being justly condemned for many centuries of hatred and violence towards Jews, Muslims and other Godfearing people. And a large amount of recent Christian art shows that the understanding of the crucifixion as the martyrdom of God in a world filled with hatred and violence can inspire an image which is like an iron nail invading flesh. It disturbs, it connects with contemporary experience, and it penetrates deeply into people who are far less moved by any image of Christ as a stern-faced emperor or as a calm hero on a tree in a beautiful country-side.

However, that interpretation of the cross must lack credibility unless it is also affirmed and believed that this particular death was, and is, unique because it had, and has, divine as well as human power, demonstrated by the glorious resurrection of the victim. Only then can we begin to see how 'God in Christ' became the victor over evil. We do not then meet Christ as the agent of God's just wrath: we see him as the agent of God's patient love which wins in the end because, more than our own loves, it 'bears all things, believes all things, hopes all things, endures all things' (1 Corinthians 13:7).

And this love for which the cross is a placard can transform our own loves or own inability to love, if only we believe with our whole being that we actually are loved by our Creator who is also our Judge, and loved as we are and unconditionally. Often our loves are feeble because we hold ourselves back, fearing to be exposed and hurt. Here we are confronted by the God who by embodiment is entirely human, entirely exposed (in historical reality, naked in helpless agony), and entirely rejected by those who crucify. We must, and can, learn from that to give ourselves away – to him. And often we find it impossible to offer to anyone total love because in our childhood we did not experience it. One of the great contributions of modern psychology to self-understanding has been its demonstration that a coldly unloving parent, or rejection or physical abuse when young, can cripple any man or woman unless an even stronger experience can unlock the innate capacity to love. Even when childhood has been survived without that abuse, later suffering may make it almost impossible to believe that the world is governed by a good God. And even if adult life is survived without acute suffering, there can still be acute awareness of the suffering of other people and of other creatures; there can still be 'sympathy' which means fellow-suffering. For all the miserable and all the sympathetic, what is needed most is some assurance that the Creator of all loves all, more passionately than any parent or lover. The essential message of Christ's cross may therefore be put in English words of one syllable: he died to show us that God loves us and pays the price of love.

We have seen that Jesus was more than a teacher of spiritual wisdom as the Gnostics maintained, developing elaborate theories about the secrets which he revealed in order that a small circle might escape from the material world. He was also more than a man whom God decided to make divine (Adoptionism), and more than God looking like a man but not really being one (Docetism). He was more than an 'angel' (which means 'messenger') and the Letter to the Hebrews had to begin by insisting on this. He was more than one god among many, although Pliny the Younger reported to the Roman emperor that the Christians sang hymns 'as to a god'. And he was more than a unique divine being created by God: the Church had to insist on this in the long battle against Arianism. He was the one true God present and active in a real man. But how was that possible? And how could this 'incarnation' be related to other ways or 'modes' in which God had made himself known to Christians – as the Creator of the universe and as the Spirit inspiring many humans?

A theological movement (Monarchianism or Modalism) was rejected because in its determination to affirm the unity of God as the single monarch it could be thought to be saying that the Father was crucified, that the Son was never a real man and that the Holy Spirit's work was in no way distinct. But modern theologians have been more impressed, thinking that this movement's real fault was to be too philosophical, rather than stressing that what we can know about the divine reality is the divine activity – the approach preferred in the Bible, where God frequently acts but does not reveal himself completely. When Moses asks him what he is, he is told to mind his own business (Exodus 3:14). When Moses asks him to show how he moves and works, he is allowed no more than a glimpse of his back (Exodus 33:23).

However, the doctrines which became orthodoxy can also be criticised as being too theoretical, and that fault can be seen in the fact that the creeds which emerged from the bishops' councils held in Nicaea in 325 and Constantinople in 381 did not mention any activity between the birth of Jesus and his death. It would also have been both more biblical and more realistic had the bishops' decisions not been followed by disputes distracting the Church from tasks which could rightly be called Christlike – tasks of service and evangelism, urgently needed then as now. These controversies gradually got more involved in the language of Greek philosophy which Jesus never knew, and their decrees were enforced by the imperial police, in the Roman tradition which crucified him. That left a terrible legacy.

The orthodoxy which emerged from Nicaea and its sequels was full of philosophical terms which would have bewildered Jesus and the early Christians. Thus the Father, the Son and the Spirit are equally divine, equal in power and honour, united by *ousia* (substance or being), but each has an identity, an *hypostasis* (which originally meant 'basis') or *prosopon* (which originally meant 'mask'). Unfortunately the last two terms have been translated as 'person' (through the Latin *persona*), which adds more to the identity than was intended – so that the doctrine of the Trinity has often been misunderstood as talk about three gods, which of course was never the intention but was the inevitable outcome, with disastrous consequences for the Christian mission to other believers in the ultimate unity of God.

At Chalcedon in 451 it was decided that while on earth Christ had two natures, divine and human, 'without confusion, change, division or separation'. Not without reason, in modern times it has been doubted whether natures which cannot be identified apart from each other can be two. Such doubt has also questioned the speculation that God the Son 'assumed' human nature but not a human personality. There has been a similar reaction to the bishops' decision in 680 that Jesus had two wills. Equally difficult to defend is the decision of Spanish bishops in 589 that the Holy Spirit proceeded 'from the Son' as well as 'from the Father' as in the creed of 381. The papacy resisted this addition for another four hundred years but yielded eventually, bowing to the feeling that no compliment to the Son could be excessive. But this concession increased the split with the Eastern Orthodox and in recent discussion it has become clear that were the creed of 381 ever to be revised (which at present is an impossibility), its insistence that the Father is the ultimate source of all divine activity could be safeguarded by an agreement that the Spirit is given 'through the Son'.

The conclusions to these theological controversies may also be criticised from a more mundane viewpoint. Many of the European tribesmen who followed their kings into baptism also followed them into an Arian interpretation of the mystery of Christ (if they ever thought about it), and the division between Catholic and Arian weakened the Church in the West, to the extent that the Muslim invaders of Spain had what was almost literally a walk-over triumph. Similarly in the East Muslim conquerors were initially welcomed by 'heretical' (Monophysite) Christians as being better than control by the emperors in Constantinople. Initially other 'heretics' (Nestorians) were welcomed in Persia precisely because they were unpopular in Constantinople, but later the Mongols massacred them and even knowledge about them disappeared almost completely because other Christians did not care about their fate. And the controversy about 'and the Son' (*Filioque*) was a factor in the schism between the Eastern and Western Churches in Europe. That schism greatly weakened any hope that Christendom might present a united front against the victorious Turks. It has also greatly damaged all later development both in Catholicism and in Orthodoxy, just as in western Europe both Catholicism and Protestantism have been badly hurt by their separation. A saying preserved by Mark (3:24) supplies a commentary: 'If a kingdom is divided against itself, that kingdom cannot stand.'

Instead of venerating these overambitious and divisive definitions of the uniqueness of Jesus, in our own time it seems far more meaningful to say simply that Jesus was not a person in the ordinary modern sense before the process called birth, yet his human existence was utterly unique. Not only was he uniquely gifted, in that no teacher has been so widely remembered and no leader has been so deeply influential. Christians also wish to say that his life was intended by the eternal Creator of all that exists. In two of the gospels this faith was expressed by saying that he was conceived by the power of the Holy Spirit and in John's by saying that he was the embodiment of the divine Word, and it must still be affirmed strongly that this life was no accident.

By sharing our human nature Jesus became a 'person' as we normally use that term, completely sharing human experience both in its strengths and in its limitations. He was limited in his knowledge of science, history and other subjects, as everyone else was. But his greatest strength was that he knew God through prayer, so that he was incapable of feeling the alienation from God which is called 'sin'; even his cry of despair from the cross (a cry which no Christian would have dared to invent) was a prayer quoted from Scripture. Presumably he has remained a human person in heaven, as he promised others they would remain. But that eternal person is full of God completely with all the limitations of mortal humanity removed, and so is uniquely able to bring very imperfect humans into the bliss which he now shares with the Father. That is taught in the letter to the Hebrews, with its vision of Christ as the uniquely holy priest praying sympathetically for the unholy because he has never ceased to be human himself, remembering that he had been 'in every respect tested as we are' before being 'made perfect'. 'Since he always lives to make intercession for them', he is 'able for all time to save those who approach God through him' (7:25).

~

SIX

YES TO THE SPIRIT

For many people in the modern world 'spirituality', however under-stood, is more interesting than 'religion'. The one seems an important part of how one chooses to live and it brings known benefits, while the other seems to be an organised and traditional way of worship which addresses a deity who is remote and has no strong influence on the behaviour of worshippers. The religious institutions seem out of touch with reality, but most people are not complete materialists and it is possible to develop a do-it-yourself alternative. In practice this usually means making time to think about the things that really matter and to enter the peace which ought to be at the heart of busyness. It helps to reflect how small one's worries and ambitions are in comparison with the grandeur of nature and the mystery of its Source. One may be helped by listening to music, or by dancing, or by other ancient prac-tices to empty the mind of trivialities, or by being in a garden, or by going for a walk, or simply by sitting still. The concentration of the mind with deep breathing may lead eventually to the mystical experi-ence when the self is glad to be overwhelmed. And of course this mystical element is usually linked closely with morality as one seeks to be 'better' in every sense.

But there is a sinister side to some modern or postmodern spirit-uality. It is advocated as 'getting in touch with your real self', but that may mean in practice becoming even more self-centred than before: there may be little connection with mundane duties to family and society, or with the world's problems. Indeed, there may be little connection with reality. The plentiful literature about 'Mind, Body and Spirit' includes a large amount of material placed in that category because it consists of stories or theories about happenings which have one feature in common: they have no link with reputable science, let alone with intellectually respectable religion. They are the 'superstition' or 'magic' against which science and religion can be allied, and so far from affirming human dignity in an age of materialism, they can reduce the ability to relate to, and cope with, the world as experienced when not in some kind of trance, which may be inspired by ultimately destructive drugs.

In more traditional societies spirituality may not take the form of reaching out to one's deeper self: to people whose identity is given by belonging to a family and a wider group that may seem the depth of individualism. Such people will probably take the reality of the spirit world for granted, so that their age-old spirituality may be called 'spiritism' by bemused moderns. They may long to be in contact with the dead who are still loved, or may feel the need to appease living spirits whose power, often hostile, is at least semi-divine. Although belief in the Creator is also seldom questioned, the 'high God' may seem too grand and too supernatural to need or deserve much worship, and it may seem more practical to concentrate on the spirits of ancestors, or on spirits felt to be in nature, or on gods known about because of a story held sacred in one's group.

Because in a more traditional society life is often less busy but also less protected from disaster, these strong spirits may be feared. Offended ancestors can inflict punishment, much as hostile neighbours may cast spells. A spirit at work in nature can easily damage or kill. A god known through the tribe's tradition can be aggressively evil, perhaps causing a fatal disease. So 'spirituality' in this sense can mean placating invisible enemies. However, a spirit less than the supreme 'God' can also be deeply loved. In 'Hindu' – which means Indian – spirituality many hundreds of gods can be named but love can be given to the playful, wise and generally attractive Lord Krishna, regarded as one of the many incarnations of the 'high' God worshipped as Vishnu. In the Northern Buddhist tradition love very close to worship may be given to humans who postponed their entry into the final bliss because of their compassion for humans still trapped in this life. In the Orthodox or Catholic version of Christianity veneration and love may go from the heart to a saint, in particular to Mary the 'God-bearer' or 'mother of God'.

But for Christians the supremely significant spirit is the divinely Holy Spirit, celebrated in the Bible as the ultimate source of any vitality thought to be admirable – and of any creativity. Eight psalms eloquently praise the activity of this Spirit throughout nature (8, 65, 93, 104, 139, 147, 148) and others including 139 affirm magnificently the ability of this Spirit to reach and rescue anyone anywhere. From first to last the New Testament declares this Spirit's unique presence and power in the life and work of Jesus. The image of the Spirit descending 'like a dove' at his baptism seems curiously inadequate (Mark 1:10), but 'the Spirit immediately drove him out into the wilderness', Mark adds – and into the whole of his driven life, until the cross. When the scribes came down from Jerusalem and said about this provincial healer 'by the ruler of the demons he casts out demons', Jesus is said to have exploded: 'whoever blasphemes against the Holy Spirit can never have forgiveness, but is guilty of an eternal sin' (Mark 3:22–30). Presumably this was because they had called healing demonic, confusing sheer goodness with sheer evil. To Jesus, the 'arm of the Lord', uplifted so often in the history of his people, had become the 'finger of God' creating the kingdom of God through healing (Luke 11:20), because he applied to himself a prophet's conviction that 'the Spirit of the Lord is upon me' (Luke 4:18). To Paul the new power in prayers and lives was such that the Spirit does the praying, if need be 'with sighs too deep for words' (Romans 8:26) – and the Spirit also does the living, so that a Christian's body becomes a temple of the Holy Spirit and a Christian community the Spirit-filled new embodiment of Christ (1 Corinthians 6:19, 12:27). And many millions alive today would say the same. This is the biggest factor in the spread of Christianity in modernising Africa, for example.

The Holy Spirit believed in by Christians is therefore said to be like the wind which 'blows where it chooses, and you hear the sound of it, but you do not know where it comes from or where it goes' (John 3:8). It is not like looking down a well and finding at the bottom a face which is one's deeper self. On the contrary, it takes one out of one's self. It can arrive like the desert wind which whips the sand up into a pillar and the excitement produced can be higher than anything known in any other setting. It can be sudden like lightning and set someone on fire with a mission. Or it can light up the whole landscape of life because now one can see a good meaning in it all. Or it can come more quietly and slowly like the dawn, bringing the sunshine of steady happiness. Or it can inspire joy when God in his bliss seems more real than oneself. Or it can bring steadfastness to keep prayer and work going in a time of dark desolation in heart and mind. This inexhaustible energy which is the gift of the eternal God is so much the best source of vitality, creativity and patient courage that it can seem puzzling that not everyone sees that this spirituality is the best on offer – puzzling, until it is realised that some Christians have claimed that the Holy Spirit makes them infallible, prefers to be accompanied by spectacular miracles, and does not operate outside Christianity. These claims are now so often rejected as being fantastic, naive or conceited that it has become urgently necessary to attempt to say what Christians have really experienced.

In the second of two letters said to have been written by Peter it is claimed that 'no prophecy of scripture is a matter of one's own interpretation, because no prophecy ever came by human will, but people moved by the Holy Spirit spoke from God' (1:20, 21). This has often been interpreted as the Bible teaching that it is infallible, inerrant or at least trustworthy. Yet despite the claim that its author was an eyewitness to the transfiguration of Jesus on the mountain (1:16–18), almost all scholars are now agreed that the letter cannot have been written by the apostle. One reason given is that its style and tone are very different from the First Letter of Peter, but there also Petrine authorship is usually now rejected. Taking the name of a revered leader, because trying to teach as he would have done or had taught his disciples to do, was a practice more acceptable in the ancient world than it would be today – but it is still not a reason why a modern reader should believe that this 'forger' was himself divinely inspired to speak nothing but the truth. The fact that the author heaps personal abuse on teachers whom he regards as false, rather than reporting and discussing what they have actually said, will also not be regarded as one of his credentials.

He ends by admitting that in Paul's letters there are 'some things hard to understand, which the ignorant and unstable twist to their own destruction, as they do other scriptures' (3:15, 16), although again there is no discussion about any passage said to have been twisted. That treatment of the letters as 'scripture' has led most scholars to think that 2 Peter was written almost a hundred years after the deaths of Peter and Paul. It overlaps with another letter also now treated as scripture, claiming to come from Jude 'the brother of James', presumably James the brother of Jesus. But modern readers need not believe that every word in either letter is the word of God. That even applies to Paul's authentic letters, and it is plainly not true that all the predictions to be read in the Hebrew Bible were 'from God', because many of them were proved wrong by events.

It can be demonstrated beyond reasonable doubt that the Bible includes errors and superseded teachings, as is inevitable in literature written over more than a thousand years and completed almost two thousand years ago. 2 Peter is an extreme example of the difference between ancient and modern views of what is authentic and authoritative in religious writing, but many other examples could be given. To give one: the quotations in the New Testament from what Christians call the Old Testament would not be accepted in serious modern discussion, for they are made with little regard for the original context and language (they usually quote from the Greek translation of the Hebrew). Matthew's gospel includes two well-known examples of misunderstanding (1:23, 21:5). Very few people then had ready access to the very bulky Hebrew Bible (neither Jesus nor Paul can have carried one around with him) and it seems that the early Christians used lists of prophecies they thought appropriate for use in arguments, with no comparison of author with author and period with period. And for a long time Christians were uncertain about which books should be revered as the New Testament: the first undisputed list dates from 376. Agreement about the exact contents of the Old Testament also proved difficult. The Bible in Hebrew was more firmly defined when Judaism was reconstructed after AD 70, but Greek-reading Jews accepted other books which were also used in Christian teaching and worship. These were rejected by the Protestant Reformers but included in Holy Scripture for Catholics by the Council of Trent in 1548. They can be called 'Apocrypha'.

Evidently the gift of *ta biblia* (the books) carries with it the plea that we should use our brains, also God's gift, on their variety of date, style, purpose and importance. So it may be asked whether it is wise to say in church that a biblical passage is always 'the word of the Lord'. If one aims in modern times at an honest use of Scripture, however, one can still affirm that when its books are taken together, the Christian Bible has a message, 'living and active, sharper than any two-edged sword' and well 'able to judge the thoughts and intentions' of any human reader or hearer (Hebrews 4:12). For a Christian this will be truer about the New Testament than about the Old and so the gratitude for the New must be special. Again almost endless examples could be given, but we may return to 2 Peter. If it dates from around AD 150, it was written at a time when the Christian movement had many reasons to be depressed. The Easter appearances had ceased; the early followers of Jesus had died; Jerusalem had been demolished; Jews no longer had a country of their own but had their own strengthened religion that excluded Christianity; Christians were persecuted, poor and not very numerous; they found it more difficult than ever to forgive those who mistreated them; and although the great idea of the rapid coming of God's kingdom to cover the earth had often been reduced to hope for the return from heaven of Jesus as Judge of a mostly evil world, Jesus had never returned in that sense. Many were asking 'Where is the promise of his coming? For all things continue as they were from the beginning of creation!' And to this a positive reply could be made and could convince: 'With the Lord a thousand years are like one day. The Lord is patient with you but will come like a thief', without warning (2 Peter 3:3–10). That surely was the word of the Lord, whoever spoke it.

In the twentieth century the Pentecostal and (less organised) Charismatic movements developed on an immense scale because they were inspired by definite experiences believed to be direct contacts with God and proofs of the power of the Holy Spirit. These experiences have had much in common. In response to preaching, or sometimes to private talk or to reading the Bible, there was conversion. This could lead to intense prayer, to weeping over sins, or to ecstatic joy and confidence. In the release of emotion people could jerk or twist, or be 'slain' as they fell to the ground. They could speak in a special way, in 'tongues' which could be thought to be languages they had never learned. This would be a 'baptism in the Spirit' whether or not there had been an earlier baptism in water and whether or not water-baptism received in infancy was now thought to be so inadequate that the adult convert felt guided to seek baptism again, preferably by immersion as a symbol of death and resurrection. Then these 'born again' Christians could be 'saints' in some sense and 'apostles' too, as they felt morally compelled and powerfully commissioned to be evangelists, often expecting further 'signs' as miracles of the kind recorded in the Acts of the Apostles.

The past tense has been used about a major phenomenon shaping Christianity in its twentieth century, but of course growth did not stop in AD 2000. However, hesitations or criticisms by fellow Christians have also never stopped. 'Charismatics' have welcomed the definite *charisma* or gift of the Spirit but have not felt any obligation to be highly emotional or recruited into a different congregation. Although Pentecostalists have sincerely seen themselves as loyally reviving the 'apostolic faith' which ought to be authoritative for all Christians, conservative and liberal Christians alike have often been suspicious or hostile. They have thought, and sometimes said, that the preaching can be manipulative and the response to it hysterical. If 'speaking in tongues' is claimed to be the ability to speak other people's languages miraculously, critics have found the claim unconvincing. If it is claimed to be speech not in any orderly language, critics have agreed that this may be a part of the experience of some people touched by the Spirit, but they have seen great danger in any conclusion that this 'Spirit baptism' results in a superior kind of Christian. Critics have noted that many schisms have resulted, both within previously existing churches and in the Pentecostal movement itself, when the New Testament's repeated insistence on unity 'in the Spirit' seems to have been ignored.

Even Pentecostalists and Charismatics have differed in their claims about the sanctification which results from an experience which, they maintain, is a blessing bestowed by God when it is sorely needed. Does it always or usually bring physical healing? Does it bring wealth as well as health? Does it bring the power to 'prophesy' with predictions or exceptionally wise insights? Is it a 'finished work' or does it need 'shepherding' for a long time by an authoritative pastor or prophet? Does it involve more faithful membership of a traditional church, or a move to a new denomination or a 'house church'? Does it involve an end to racism or nationalism, or a church more closely identified with one race and one nation? Does it involve fundamentalism, or some kind of Spirit-guided selectivity when reading the Bible? And does it lead to more miracles as 'signs and wonders'? If so, should these be made public?

It can seem that the traditional concerns of 'liberalism' have very little connection with these experiences or with a serious discussion of their significance, but a truly liberal response will surely be close to a properly conservative one. The reality of these Christian experiences must be acknowledged, although it may be added that there are parallels in other religions and even in some gatherings for purposes not religious. It must be confessed that the popularity of this kind of Christianity is currently a verdict on the boredom induced by much ordinary church life. And it must be hoped that people who disagree outside or within the Pentecostal and Charismatic movements will admit the truth that from the beginning Christians have felt free to differ about what is not essential. In the long run this has been one of the strengths of Christianity, enabling it to take root in an astonishing variety of soils.

The New Testament says plainly that the first generation of Christians was far from perfect and far from completely united, despite the joy, courage and energy which bear witness to the energising reality of the risen Jesus and the given Spirit. This fact emerges in the Acts of the Apostles, all the more significantly because the author is so convinced about the power of the Spirit that this history might be named the Acts of the Spirit.

In the fourth gospel (20:19–23) the disciples first receive the Spirit in a quiet and private scene during the evening of the first Easter Day and no mention is made of their reactions. That may well reflect true history, for the appearances of Jesus must have been understood as a new mode of his presence, with a spiritual power which was greater than his everyday physical presence had been, but which was not dramatic or public. For the author of Acts, however, the promise is that 'you will receive power' (1:8) and weeks pass before that power is poured out dramatically and in public. Then there is a sound 'like the rush of a violent wind', 'tongues as of fire' make the apostles speak in languages they have never learned, and people think them drunk (2:1–15) – which is odd, for intoxicated people are seldom eloquent in languages they have not studied. The promise to the people is that if they are baptised they too will receive 'the gift of the Holy Spirit' (2:8).

Later, when this promise is fulfilled again, another house will be shaken (4:31). Even before baptism this spectacular gift can be unmistakable (11:44–48). The question is asked about a definite experience: 'Did you receive the Holy Spirit when you became believers?' (19:2). The Spirit is poured out again on Stephen as he lectures the Sanhedrin about the sin of 'opposing the Holy Spirit' (7:51), on Philip who is 'snatched away' by the Spirit after converting the Ethiopian civil servant (8:39), on the Gentiles who received the Spirit as it 'fell upon' them (10:44–48), on Paul who is 'forbidden by the Holy Spirit' to avoid crossing over to Europe (16:6–10).

Yet Luke, dramatist as he is, does not conceal facts which show that the problems of Christians were not ended dramatically. Initially the Christians 'devoted themselves to the apostles' teaching and fellowship, to the breaking of bread and the prayers' and 'had all things in common', so that in the power of the Spirit 'many signs and wonders were done among the people' (2:42, 44, 5:12). That was Paradise. But it has to be confessed that Paradise was soon lost. The road ahead of the little human community in Jerusalem became 'the Way' (Acts 19:9, 24:22), and it took Christians through many adventures, problems and novelties with accompanying disagreements. In detailed modern studies of Acts this reality has now emerged despite its author's evident wish to gloss over differences. For example, he claims that soon after his conversion and escape from Damascus Paul returned to Jerusalem. He was commended to the Christians by the much respected Barnabas and moved freely among the apostles and the citizens (9:23–30). But in his letter to the Galatians Paul affirmed 'before God' that after his conversion three years in Damascus or Arabia passed before this visit, when he saw only two of the apostles and was unknown to other Christians in Judea (1:15–24). He relied on his own meeting with Christ, not on any conference.

According to Acts Paul returned to Jerusalem not long after (11:30), but he told the Galatians that it was 'after fourteen years' (2:1). Even in Acts his disappointment at his cool reception in the mother church is hinted at, for when Barnabas becomes leader of the church in Antioch he has to seek out Paul, who has returned to his native city, Tarsus. If Barnabas had not been 'full of the Holy Spirit' (11:24), presumably Paul would have spent the rest of his life as perhaps the best maker of tents in Tarsus. Yet in Acts we are told that he had been convinced of his call to lead a mission to the Gentiles during his conversion (26:17–18) – and that this call had been confirmed during a vision in Jerusalem, in the temple itself (22:17–21). What seems clear is that after the conversion there was a long period (a dozen years?) of uncertainty and waiting – Paul's Nazareth and wilderness.

But who wrote 'Luke' and Acts? Acts includes without explanation some passages recording how 'we' travelled with Paul and these narratives dominate the book from 16:10 onwards. They have supported the tradition that the author was 'Luke the beloved physician' mentioned in letters at least connected with Paul (Colossians 4:14; 2 Timothy 4:11), and the travel diaries may well be the work of that amiable doctor. He would also have had the education needed to write the whole of Acts, yet that history does not reproduce Paul's own version of events or his distinctive theology, so that it would seem that he had no access to Paul's letters. Perhaps he knew his body better than his mind? And perhaps the author of 'Luke' and of most of Acts has much in common with the author of the fourth gospel: we do not know their names, they preserved some historical facts, they had a real insight into the new spiritual life in the power of the spirit, and they told stories brilliantly.

The story in Acts of the apostles' experience during the festival of Pentecost has been used to support the 'Pentecostal' claim that the most important gift of the Spirit is the ability to speak in 'tongues'. But Acts says the gift to the apostles was of the ability to speak without learning the native languages of 'devout Jews living in Jerusalem', having come from many different places outside the land of Israel. And there are problems about this story: not only is the miracle improbable (although claims have been made that it has been repeated), but it was also not necessary, since residents in Jerusalem could presumably speak either Aramaic or Greek. These were the only two languages known to have been used by (for example) Paul, although it would have been very useful to be able to communicate miraculously with country folk. It therefore seems probable that the author's purpose was to dramatise the inspiration of the eventual mission to Gentiles living alongside Jews in cities in the Roman empire, which had in it the potential to become a mission to 'all nations' (as in Matthew 28:19).

What occurred during the festival of Pentecost was, it seems, what may be called babbling in excitement (*glossolalia*): there we have a fact. But in his first letter to them Paul pleaded to the Christians in Corinth to broaden their understanding of what had been given. He does not mention the miracle recounted in Acts but wisdom, knowledge, faith, the powers to heal, to work miracles and to 'prophesy' – all are gifts of the Spirit and may be given to different people in different measures. Paul values most the powers to love other people and to pray, speak and sing 'with the mind' as well as the spirit. 'I would rather speak five words with my mind, in order to instruct others also, than ten thousand words in a tongue' (14:19). It seems that he shared this attitude with his Lord, for nowhere in the gospels is Jesus said to have spoken in words without meaning: a prayer when he 'rejoiced in the Holy Spirit' is entirely lucid (Luke 10:24). And it is not a prayer of thanksgiving that his disciples have become so wise that they understand deep secrets, as the Gnostic gospels are to claim: these disciples have seen what is hidden from 'the wise', Satan falling from power like a 'flash of lightning', because Galilean villagers have been healed.

It seems possible to compare the disputes which troubled the first generation of Christians with the controversies which divide Christians some two thousand years later. The first big question was how the little Christian community in Jerusalem could accommodate recruits who spoke only Greek, without Aramaic. When daily rations are distributed to Greek-speaking widows in ways announced only in Aramaic, they complain and the apostles have to appoint seven deputies with Greek names (6:16). The perfect unity of 'the apostles' fellowship' has been broken.

In Acts 15 this eirenic author gives a detailed account of a council or conference in Jerusalem where the apostles and elders of that mother church agree with Barnabas and Paul (in that order) and send out a decree that 'it has seemed good to the Holy Spirit and to us' that Gentile converts should be obliged to abstain from meat which has been sacrificed to idols or has blood still in it, and from sexual immorality. By implication converts are not obliged to be circumcised or to keep the rest of the Jewish religion. The agreement has been eased by Peter, who in Acts 10 has already ordered the baptism of uncircumcised but Spirit-filled Gentiles. But in his surviving letters Paul does not mention this council or its decree. Instead he tells the Galatians that he had a 'private meeting' with three leaders in Jerusalem who asked 'only one thing, that I should remember the poor' (2:1–10).

He immediately adds that when back in Antioch he opposed Peter 'to his face' and 'before them all', accusing him of hypocrisy. He was furious that although Peter did not live 'like a Jew' himself, he had ceased to share the food of Gentile Christians when instructed by 'people from James' (2:11–14). The author of Acts does not mention this quarrel, instead claiming that Paul himself always kept the Jewish food laws (21:24). Paul does mention that Barnabas took Peter's side in Antioch, but he does not add that after this quarrel he ceased to be a missionary commissioned by that church.

A fact which emerges from these rival accounts about disputes is that the problems connected with Gentile Christianity went deep. The apostles in control were Jews whose tendency would nowadays be called

'conservative', but Paul was something of a 'liberal', a scholar, an original thinker and an independent by temperament, reaching out to a
wider world. In this tense situation any agreement which might be
reached was interpreted differently by people with different personali-
ties who maintained different positions. We can see that the modern
problems outlined earlier in this book are not without precedent.
Indeed, there is a parallel between the controversy about circumcision
as a qualification for full membership of the Church and the current
debate about the maintenance of traditional roles for the two genders
and the keeping of traditional rules in sexual morality. Two thousand
years ago it seemed very important in the Gentile world that the male
sexual organ should not be mutilated; there were very few statues of
nude women but many of men, including emperors, displaying this
organ which women lacked. On the other hand, male circumcision was
the badge of Judaism; Jesus and all the men who had followed him in
the early days were circumcised in obedience to that law; and it is not
surprising that his brother James and many other Jews assumed that
anyone wishing to join what was still a Jewish movement honouring
Jesus would conform to this requirement believed to date back to
Abraham (Acts 7:8). But today the penis is thought to be interesting in
other connections. Similarly there is a link between the controversy
about eating meat with the blood still in it, as was normal for the
Gentiles, and current disputes about Christian behaviour. Paul allowed
the practice provided that the host did not mention that the animal had
been sacrificed in a pagan temple (1 Corinthians 8), yet according to
Acts the apostles had corporately and strictly prohibited such a viola-
tion of the law of Moses. Again, the problem now seems remote. It
seems that the Holy Spirit did not end these disputes dramatically and
rapidly, but eventually did inspire reactions to further events.

One event was the decline and fall of Jerusalem as the mother church
of Christianity. Initially the communism which pooled all financial
resources meant that Christians such as Galilean fishermen could survive without jobs in a city which depended on its temple in economics
as well as religion, but the capital raised was consumed, membership
grew but jobs did not, and the result was the poverty which made James
beg Paul to raise funds, and made Paul devote much of his energy to this
managerial and difficult task. All the Christians had to leave the city,
which had become the headquarters of the disastrous rebellion. Some
returned and there was a line of bishops, but the Vatican was to be built
elsewhere.

What had been orthodoxy when Jerusalem was still the Christian
centre, before 'Matthew' and 'Luke' wrote their gospels, may be seen in
the Letter of James. This was included in the New Testament in the

belief that its author was the well-known brother of Jesus, and this seems possible although it is written in elegant Greek (which may be the work of a scribe). But the teaching is that of a Jew who taught other Jews and concentrated on practical morality as 'a servant of God and of the Lord Jesus Christ'. He loftily ignored new ideas about circumcision and the food laws and confined his consideration of Pauline theology to the observation that 'faith without works is dead' (3:26). When urging patience under suffering he recommended the example not of Jesus but of Job (5:11). It seems likely that his Christology was that which we see in the early chapters of Luke's gospel and of Acts: 'a man attested to you by God', now 'exalted to the right hand of God' (2:22, 23). But the letters to the Colossians and Ephesians, probably in their present form the work of disciples of Paul, went beyond this, as we have seen – and the future lay with that higher Christology, when a Jewish form of Christianity could be condemned as heretical.

It was to be a future with more discipline, especially in the enforcement of doctrines about Christ and of uniformity in worship. The letters to Timothy and Titus, also probably written in their present form by Paul's disciples, provide some evidence. Disorder such as Paul had tried to control in Corinth without any resident deputy was now to be disciplined by an overseer (*episkopos*) or bishop.

He should 'proclaim the message' taking into account the Hebrew Scriptures which are not as binding as James had believed, but are still 'useful for teaching, for reproof, for correction and for training in righteousness' (2 Timothy 3:16). Previously Paul had been able to do no more than plead that everything in the Corinthian church should be done 'decently and in order', but now the Spirit had given Timothy 'a spirit of power and of love and of self-discipline', and the emphasis in these letters is on the power of the bishop to teach sound doctrine and to rebuke any whose morals are unsound. The Spirit gets few mentions. As sociologists have pointed out, Christianity, which had been charismatic, became institutional – and able to survive. But we may ask: survive to what purpose?

According to Acts 18:2 Paul was working in Corinth when brought before Gallio the local governor. That was in the summer of AD 51, a date known because a dated inscription has been found also naming this Roman official. It is the only certain date in the life of Paul and it seems that he took the funds he had raised to Jerusalem six years later, only to be arrested by the Romans for causing a riot among Jews and finding little or no support from the Christians there (who, however, presumably took the money). Acts ends not with his martyrdom but with him teaching in Rome 'with all boldness and without hindrance'. Yet centuries would follow when Eastern Orthodoxy and Roman

Catholicism, while honouring him, would be systems rather different from his own emphasis on a personal and Spirit-filled relationship with Jesus as Lord. Eventually, in the sixteenth century, that emphasis returned in Protestant and Catholic Reformations and it has been at the centre of all vitality in modern Christianity, whether conservative or liberal. But all this took time.

Today it seems almost inconceivable that Paul was so deeply involved in controversies about circumcision and food laws, and that his gospel returned to the centre amid controversies about other issues which now look equally strange. So it seems possible that in the future new ideas about gender and sexual morality – ideas which horrified him when he met their ancient equivalents – will be more often tolerated by the leadership in the churches and eventually accepted, as they are already accepted in quiet practice by many millions who identify themselves as Christians. However, it is not the situation as I write. What seems realistic is to hope that while the debates are pursued vigorously some of the best words of Paul, in his day not one to pull his punches, will be remembered. The longest lasting harvest of diversity is 'love, joy, peace, kindness, generosity, faithfulness, gentleness and self-control' (Galatians 5:22). And that reception of the Spirit given to the Christian Church could impress many who now stand outside.

Just as we live in the first age which has known the extent and origin of the physical universe, so we live in the first age to have anything like an appreciation of another phenomenon – a universe of undeniably genuine, rich and creative experience and aspiration, the spiritual and religious life of humankind. And it seems reasonable to believe that all this splendour has a single origin, the Spirit or energy of the Reality whose name in English is God. Not only Christians can now be heard telling some of the truth about the mystery of God, and goodness, often understood in the same way everywhere, can be found everywhere. This recognition of facts and experience has been called the Copernican revolution in religion because it sees the faiths on Earth as being like planets all moving around the one sun, and this comparison may be even more illuminating if developed. Some people now try to look at the sun directly, but that can be a disaster because human eyes have not been made to see God. More people have tried to bask in the sun without any man-made clothes, but that too is dangerous because human skin has not been made trouble-free: thinking or talking about God needs words and images which are usually supplied by a tradition. The wisest course seems to be to live in the light one has and to learn from other light. This applies to Christians who do not worship their own tradition on a Sunday.

The first witness to be called in defence of the claim that others beside Christians 'feel after and find' God is Paul, the most articulate ambassador ever of the faith in 'Christ crucified'. Not only do we have reconstructions of the sort of thing Paul might say to Gentiles about their search for God and their experience of his goodness through the goodness of nature. Repeatedly he insists that it is God's purpose to show mercy to all. We also have his own words about what his fellow Jews had been given by God: 'the adoption, the glory, the covenants, the giving of the law, the worship and the promises' (Romans 9:4). It is taught in Scriptures received by Christians as well as Jews that the Spirit flooded from God into the patriarchs of Israel, the Hebrew prophets great and small from Moses onwards, the judges and the warrior-kings supremely, including David, the poets to whom we owe the psalms, the musicians who could stir or soothe, Samson the very strong man, Solomon the very clever man, the craftsmen gifted to create beauty for the tabernacle in the wilderness (Exodus 35:30—36:7). If 'the spirit of the Lord' rested on a leader of the Lord's people, it would give 'wisdom and understanding, counsel and might, knowledge and the fear of the Lord' (Isaiah 11:2). And if this Spirit is to be given to the whole people in 'a new covenant', it will mean that every one of them will 'know the Lord' (Jeremiah 31:34) – and know his spiritual power. It will be like a breath clothing with flesh and life the 'very many' and 'very dry' bones of a massacred army (Ezekiel 37:1–14). 'Your daughters shall prophesy, your old men shall dream dreams, and your young men shall see visions' (Joel 2:28). And if Christians can agree that the Spirit spoke to those Hebrews, and acted in them, it is not a very big step to acknowledge the presence and the power of this same Spirit in the history of every people on earth.

Certainly the Spirit was believed to have inspired the prophets of Israel to denounce the gods of surrounding peoples – the terrifying gods who embodied the power of the Egyptian state, the gods of Canaan who promised rain if stimulated by sexual orgies, the idols who demanded the sacrifice of children. Yet when a temple was built in Jerusalem the craftsmen came from outside Israel and used a design also imported, and when a tradition of 'wisdom' in scholars who were educated and sophisticated by international standards developed, they too drew materials and themes from outside their own little country. Some of the sternest of the prophets had visions of Yahweh the God of Israel blessing 'Egypt my people', the distant Ethiopians and the unpleasantly close Philistines (Isaiah 11:25; Amos 9:7). It could even be said that Cyrus the Persian had been anointed like a king of Israel and taken by the hand to work for the world's one Lord (Isaiah 45:1–7).

Because the 'Old' Testament is so firmly in the Christian Bible, some

of the early theologians of the Church taught that the Greek philosophers whom they greatly admired had somehow been Christians before
Christ (perhaps by learning from the Hebrews). A term taken from
philosophy, in Greek, and from Philo the philosophical Jew, could be
used: the divine *Logos* is the Reason which governs the universe and
enlightens humankind, and this idea can be matched by the ideas of
Wisdom and the Word in securely biblical sources. The Roman Catholic
theologian Karl Rahner modernised these boldly inclusive ideas by calling some non-Christians 'anonymous Christians', but if the ancient
terms now seem obscure, this suggestion seems open to rejection as
being both understandable and offensive. A President of the USA would
not welcome being praised as an anonymous Muslim and a pope would
not be pleased to be called an anonymous Buddhist. It seems clearer to
say, as many Christians do say nowadays, that all the goodness and wisdom in the world's great faiths are inspired by the one Spirit of the one
God.

It also seems to be a fact that the Spirit of God can work in any
person, however unlike a famous leader or teacher that person may be.
This is implied in the usually unread first chapter of Matthew's gospel,
tracing the ancestry of the carpenter who was the husband of Mary 'of
whom Jesus was born'. Three other women are mentioned as belonging
to this family tree. One is Tamar the widow who pretended to be a
prostitute in order that Judah her father-in-law should have a son.
Another is Rahab the prostitute, who hid Israel's spies from their
enemies, and the third is Ruth, the Arab refugee.

This biblical vision of the universal work of the one Spirit is different
from relying on a few passages in the New Testament which suggest that
all non-Christians reject God and are rejected by him. One text which
may be misused is taken from the reconstruction of a speech by Peter to
the Sanhedrin in Jerusalem: there is salvation only in Jesus (Acts 4:11).
But that speech follows 'salvation' in the form of a healing 'by the name
of Jesus Christ of Nazareth' and whatever may have been actually said
or done on that occasion it is not reported that it followed any discussion of the ancient faiths of Asia, about which Peter was presumably
ignorant. Christians have indeed experienced 'salvation' in its fuller
sense through Christ alone but as they have met adherents of other
religious traditions at depth – as they very seldom did before modern
times – they have discovered why the most famous account of the gift
of the Holy Spirit includes Peter's citation of the promise that 'I will
pour out my Spirit on all flesh' (Acts 2:17).

The Jesus of John, who in fact speaks on behalf of the Johannine
community, says that the 'Spirit of truth' about to be sent cannot be
seen or known by the world, which is bound to hate the new arrival

(14:17, 15:18–25). The work of the Spirit is to prove that the world is wrong (16:8–11). Accordingly, the Jesus of John does not pray for the world – only for those who 'believe' (17:9). But in the first letter of John we find a more inclusive insight. The world is wrong if it knows only 'the desire of the flesh, the desire of the eyes, the pride in riches' (as all the world's faiths would agree), yet 'everyone who loves is born of God and knows God' (2:16, 4:7). And that insight is clear in the gospels which are closer to the historical Jesus. In his parables he often compared the goodness and wisdom of Galilean villagers with the goodness and wisdom of his Father. He makes a weary shepherd carrying a dirty animal one of the most revealing images of the Eternal.

If all these are facts about what the Christians' Bible says about Jews, we may look with open eyes at what history says about the founders of other religions.

About five hundred years before Christ a Chinese sage known to the West as Confucius was involved in a civilisation which was wealthy but divided into warring petty kingdoms badly administered. He set himself to be a reforming minister in politics but as such had only a brief career. Then he became a teacher of the 'liberal' arts in order to develop civilised minds, and an exponent of a morality based on the performance of duty in the family, in the local community and in the state. Thus a life without immediate success made him the spiritual father of a great people, and he is still that today.

About a hundred years later, also in China, a book collected the sayings of wise men who advocated a wisdom deeper than the performance of duty in a society organised as a hierarchy. A greater happiness was, they taught, known by those who stayed close and uncomplainingly to the calmly unconquerable processes and rhythms of nature. The book became a scripture of Daoist spirituality which developed tough practices in order to free the mind from distractions coming from sources less than nature. By going with the flow of nature a practitioner could reach a kind of immortality by absorption into it, like a fish returning to water.

Confucians and Daoists have not been clearly separated in the spiritual life of China and have not attacked popular beliefs in gods or spirits, but the original teaching was clear: such beings should be both honoured and kept at a distance. Siddartha Gautama (the Buddha), born into a rich Indian family around 480 BC, did not deny the existence of the many Hindu deities, but in his long spiritual quest he found that they, and sacrifices offered to them, were irrelevant. The enlightenment which he experienced and offered to followers was liberation from worse evils than the absence of civilised harmony, and it was a peace which the gods could not grant. Everywhere he saw suffering, with its climax in old age, disease and death, followed by rebirth into the same kind of life which only the deluded could desire, and he promised that any human mind could be made an exit from the prison. This path through self-control to ego-extinction has been taken, or at least genuinely admired, by many hundreds of millions in the history of Asia and has fascinated many in the modern West, amid its lust and greed.

Such Asian forms of religious spirituality do not include adoration of God as one and only, but the ultimate reality of Brahman has been the highest theme of India's spiritual teachers. To them the gods are faces and all beings are in a sense embodiments of 'That' which is Being. And almost a thousand years after the birth of the Buddha a prophet appeared in Arabia whose intense faith in the unity and majesty of God proved more powerful than the worship of tribal gods and the complicated religions of the Byzantine and Persian empires. The Qur'an heard by Muhammad became the creed and law of a civilisation from the Atlantic to the Pacific, for long richer than Europe and almost as rich as China.

He was a layman – a dealer in camels who proved himself a master as politician, legislator and warrior – but he had an undeniably spiritual experience when commanded, at times over 23 years, to recite the Qur'an. At first receiving that miracle caused him anguish and isolation, and spreading it took every bit of his very great dedication and courage. His message was utterly different from the calculating materialism and paganism of the Mecca he knew. Not all of it will strike a non-Muslim as timelessly perfect, but the essential theme was the transcendence of the One God resulting in the inevitability of judgement after death, and this book's extraordinary power has given it a permanent authority so immense that Islam is a word which means 'surrender' to its revelation, the Word made words.

Each of these great teachers taught some of the truth about God – his call to dutiful behaviour and to closeness to the nature he has created, his call to eternity above all ambitions and anxieties and all suffering, his call to see his unity beneath his many faces, his call to see his majesty and his holiness as inspiration for a noble life. However, it does not follow that, once they get beyond the Golden Rule (that the neighbour must be treated as one would wish to be treated oneself), all religions remain equally true. That is non-sense, because they differ substantially in their doctrines. It ought to be possible to think that a faith and its adherents may be divinely inspired without thinking that any human exponent has been completely correct. Certainly the history of the Christian faith itself cannot be studied with any honesty without being driven to that conclusion again and again. In the fourth gospel (15:13) we read that the 'Spirit of truth' will 'guide you into all the truth', yet we have seen that this gospel is itself untrue to the facts about the historical Jesus. Repeatedly church leaders have failed to tell the truth and live as Jesus clearly taught, while ordinary Christians have behaved extraordinarily badly, as when the medieval crusaders massacred Jews and Muslims alike while using the cross as their symbol.

If present-day Christians could admit their inherited disgrace more openly, their honesty might make it a little easier for the defenders of other faiths to be self-critical. Inevitably they react against the past contempt of Christians for the majority of humankind, and in particular against the recent record of nominally Christian nations in political or economic imperialism. But self-criticism need not be a Christian monopoly. If the arrogance of Christians is admitted, it may be granted that in other religions outsiders have been regarded as infidels or as nothing but materialists. If Christians repent of ignorance or misrepresentation, it may be granted that in other religions there has not been a great desire to learn from a careful study of the Bible and the Christian tradition. If Christians have the honesty to acknowledge that some expressions of their faith have used myths, their honesty may be matched. If they confess that they have at times misrepresented God himself, it may be granted that no human tradition perfectly accounts for the Eternal. And it may be granted that Christianity is not the only religion that has been less than helpful to humanity – as when the Confucian tradition has upheld the power of an elite, or when Daoism or Buddhism has devalued this life and its constructive tasks, or when the Hindu belief in many incarnations has suggested that the wrongs done in previous lives may justify the conditions in which the poorest now live, or when the faith of Islam can be used to defend the inequality imposed on women or the brutality of terrorism. And even Judaism, Christianity's mother and victim, is imperfect when Jews who have suffered so much inflict suffering on others.

After many years of isolationism the truth may now be seen more fully. Everywhere people search and grope for God and may 'find' him although 'he is not far from each one of us' (Acts 17:27). This is the case even when God seems 'unknown' (17:22). Everywhere the divine Spirit has created holiness and beauty, love and compassion, wisdom and skill, heroic actions and humble patience. Nowhere has the Spirit made people infallible or morally flawless, by steady pressure or by a miracle.

SEVEN

YES TO GOD

W HAT CHRISTIANS HAVE said about God is not obviously all true. Today in many countries with a long Christian past many people deny the reality of God however pictured – and do so systematically, in thought and life, whether their interest is in materialism or in spirituality. Most others are reluctant to be atheists (even in secularised Europe, France, Sweden and East Germany are the only big areas where more than 20 per cent tell polls that they have 'no religion'), but the undecided are also reluctant to give God the place 'he' occupied in the past. In more traditional societies the divine is usually taken for granted together with rest of the supernatural, but alternatives to Christianity's account of God are usually dominant in the culture. In such societies it seems likely that modern education will gradually spread the modern outlook, leaving God in the position which can be assigned to him in modern societies – if not in his coffin, then in the misty background.

Amid these challenges it is curious that the Church's liturgical year does not include a festival thanking the Creator for the creation. In regular acts of worship, when the Old Testament is used congregations may hear magnificent poetry about the creation, but the eloquence comes from an age which had never looked down a microscope, up a telescope or back on evolution. When the New Testament is read a voice may be heard from Galilee about the more-than-royal glory of wild flowers but the concentration is on personal salvation, the reality of the Creator having been assumed by Jews and Gentiles alike. In our time hymns which celebrate the grandeur and beauty of nature are loved, but they very seldom refer to the billions of years which it took for nature to become what is now admired. Sermons seldom tackle the question whether God the Creator is, as a matter of fact, 'there' to be worshipped. And it can be suspected – indeed, it has often been said – that what worshippers really worship now is their 'better selves' or their family, neighbourhood or nation, and even their church as being superior to all others.

Of course it is not easy to answer the question about the reality of God unless the difficulties are ignored, but that is not a good reason for ignoring it. If God is real 'he' matters more than anything in his creation, and if he is unreal then we must all think again in a very big way. In the final analysis the reason why any religious institution flourishes is that enough people believe that at least the essentials in its religious teaching are true and, being true, are very important. Without an updated conviction about the Reality above, around and within humankind there seems to be little point in updating churches, since in a modern or modernising society other agencies can, and do, provide spirituality, moral influence, political commentary, fellowship, counselling, community service, welfare work, music, education and entertainment, and churches entirely dedicated to community use or tourism could also still conserve the past as museums. And where faith in the Creator is no longer vigorously alive, it would seem odd if a very lively interest were to be taken in Jesus, whose entire life and teaching had no foundation other than that faith. Under the impact of modernity based on science, sooner or later all religion and all morality will have to be rethought. So how can a Christian faith in God be restated credibly?

The meaning of 'faith' as a living reality may be approached by considering what is most precious to us, the love of a spouse or friend whom we can trust totally. That love is gained only if we are willing to love and be loved, with a commitment, an investment of a life, rather than a cold calculation. Only if we make that leap into uncertainty can we enter mortal life at its brief best. So if we are told that we are loved by God we may be willing to trust him – Pascal said 'gamble' – in the hope that experience before and after death will show that we have not been fools. Faith can also be understood if we reflect on what gives us self-respect. For most of us a quiet mind is possible only if on the whole we have behaved as decently as could be managed, or in old-fashioned language if we have obeyed the commands of the moral law speaking through the conscience. So we may be prepared to regard the conscience as the voice of God. But the sense of being confronted by God need not depend upon a conviction that love is the clue to what is real and good ultimately, or on a painful sensitivity to the difference between right and wrong. Any response to what seems sacred, majestic or very beautiful, or any acutely honest awareness that one is weak and mortal, can develop into a wish to know more about the Source of it all and the Force in it all.

These spiritual journeys can start far outside any community based on faith and in some societies that has now become normal. More frequent, however, is the process in which a traditional religion taught in childhood can be internalised as one's own faith. Inevitably the very young picture God as an enlargement of their (hopefully, strong and loving) parents: 'he' is the Protector who compensates for invisibility by being almighty. During adolescence adults tend to be seen as critics who do not understand the new generation, so that God can become the Judge who lays down laws which are broken for the sake of self-expression, experiments and fun. But these are not the only stages in the journey into maturity and, it may be, enlightenment. In a Jewish childhood the 'I am' of the Holy One of Israel and the good Maker of everything may have been heard; in a Muslim home the power of Allah may have been felt as bringing order to all life; after being born in India a child may have begun to explore a very rich world of imagination, devotion and wisdom. In much the same process the child of Christian parents may think of Jesus as a friend and so begin to glimpse the God who one day will be seen to suffer alongside all who suffer, who is often on the side of the outsiders, and who offers the best source of hope and healing, if need be through death. But people, rituals and stories reach young hearts quicker than any doctrine, securing new recruits for a religious tradition.

By one or other of these routes, even in a mainly secularised society it is possible to reach faith in God or at least a position in which such faith is respected. But believers are being unrealistic if they do not appreciate the force of modern secularisation, an enemy of faith never faced before in the history of religion. In a modern society all the traditional arguments for the existence of God can be regarded as temptations to embrace superstition or sentimentality instead of a factual and useful understanding of the world and of human life in it. Even in the USA many people are not only non-churchgoers: they are firm non-believers, wanting to separate Church not only from State but also from Life. In Europe the drama of secularisation has been acted out. In the eighteenth century Voltaire, so far from being a total sceptic, said that if God did not exist it would be necessary to invent him in support of morality and hope; as the nineteenth century became the twentieth the death of God could be announced as all-important news and the emotional cost could be counted; then nostalgia for the ages of faith could be replaced by joy that 'God the Father' was no longer the ultimate source of male dominance, of the sanctifying of political or economic power, or of the whole treatment of adults as children. And in the twenty-first Christian century both faith and protest may be replaced for increasing numbers by the feeling that the argument is over and God is scarcely remembered.

All these have been emotional responses to the question about God,

for or against. If we like intellectual activity we may revisit the philosophical arguments which in the past attempted to compel belief in the
reality of Reality. Nowadays it is generally agreed that not one of them
is a proof but each shows how humans have often thought, whether
they were wise or foolish. Habitually we ask 'What caused it?' and it is
not surprising that it has been thought sensible to ask what is the cause
of everything and the reason why anything exists. We also have a habit
of asking 'Will it last?' and it is no surprise that people have wanted to
ask also whether there is Something which never changes or perishes
and which exists more fully than anything we can see or touch. Such
Reality would also be greater than anything we can think or imagine,
but that has not deterred everyone from trying to think and imagine,
since this possibility can be alluring and fascinating, and famous
philosophers have encouraged thought about it.

In reply, however, it can be argued that although it might be nice to
know about God, in fact we cannot even begin to think usefully about
a being or 'Being-itself' so supreme as to be out of contact. No propo-
sition about this One can be shown to be true or false by any test: belief
will always remain belief and denial will remain denial, whatever
happens. The conclusion can be that the only sensible response to any
claim about what is really unspeakable is silence. To many modern-
minded people this total dismissal of religion, and in particular of
theology, can seem the very basis of a useful understanding of the world
and of human life in it. And once this secular challenge to religion has
been experienced at any depth, the innocence of traditional believing
cannot be recovered. The idea of God may still be held dear with
passion, or with a wistful nostalgia about years or ages of faith in the
past, but now one knows what it feels like to be without that idea.

That is a brief and superficial summary of the modern crisis of religious
faith. But today there is more to be said.

On the basis of Scripture Archbishop Ussher calculated that the
creation began on the evening of Saturday 22 October 4004 BC. He did
this in the 1650s. Even in the 1950s, when it was known that some rocks
on Earth were about 3.4 billion years old, respectable calculations did
not double that figure for the age of the universe and the generally
accepted theory was that its size has never changed very much. In the
absence of knowledge about its origin, it could be called stable or eternal. In the 1920s a mathematician who happened to be also a Roman
Catholic priest, George Lemaître, had obscurely published a theory
about its origin in a 'primeval atom', but Einstein had given the lead in
ridicule for the suggestion. In the 1930s Edwin Hubble's observations
proved that since the galaxies are moving apart the universe must be

expanding, but he had no interest in theories about its origin. When Pius XII had publicly welcomed Gamow's development of the 'primeval atom' idea, the devout Lemaître begged the Pope's advisers to discourage any further confusion between the Catholic faith, which was certainly true, and his own theory, which had been no more than one man's speculation.

It was only in 1964 that a radio telescope picked up background noise which proved that radiation from the origin could be heard on this planet as microwaves. In later scientific work the truth emerged. About 13.7 billion years ago a 'singularity' unimaginably dense, hot and small was the scene of a fluctuation which caused an explosion. At an utterly astonishing speed the history of space and time began as tiny particles resulting from minute irregularities in the 'Big Bang' got together as 'quarks' and discharged fractional amounts of electricity.

These electrons orbited around the particles called protons, producing hydrogen, the gas which constitutes almost the whole of the visible universe. Then a force of gravity neither too weak nor too strong drove atoms together, electromagnetism held them together, two joined protons made helium and stars shone. Heavier chemical elements developed, with carbon of vital importance. Generation after generation of mainly gaseous stars came and went. As they died some threw out the heavier elements which as dust or in rocks could reach the planet Earth, whose inhabitants have come to realise that the universe evolved at the right strength and speed, and with the right contents – 'right' because, amazingly, in the end what had 'happened' made our existence possible. We may have been the result of a long series of accidents but the number of necessary coincidences has been found to be very great, so that it seems common sense to regard our life as a mystery and a marvel.

A key to some understanding is called 'anthropic' because the *anthropos* (Man) whom the ancient Greeks saw as the creation's crowning glory seems to have turned out to be just that unless, unknown to us, there is some existence still more marvellous. However, to be realistic, the use of the key must be limited. It may show only that we fit into this universe because produced by it and it can also be pointed out that the universe has favoured the existence not only of us but also of a myriad of other forms of matter and life. These have been given their own existence, which may or may not be convenient to us. We like sunshine but there are also droughts, rich soil but there are also earthquakes, rain but there are also floods, fresh air but there are also hurricanes, dogs but there are also wolves, fish which fishermen sell but there are also sharks, bodies which are stunningly beautiful but there are also viruses and cancer cells – all pursuing their own objectives despite our complaints.

If we interpret science as a revelation of the work of God we have to admit that it also suggests that the Creator was pleased to create an interlocking system in which like other creatures we can suffer and die as other forms of existence function in ways which are completely natural. And if we believe that science suggests that our own existence was not completely accidental, we have to admit that almost the entire history of the universe took place before *Homo sapiens* evolved. The Creator was not impatient.

And there is a lot else which is still difficult for humans to understand. So far science has been unable to penetrate behind the original event which was nicknamed (at first dismissively) the Big Bang, and it seems that for all their wonderful abilities human brains are not well equipped to deal with what lies beyond space and time. It is difficult enough to absorb what has been recently discovered – that most of space consists of 'dark' because unobservable energy and matter, and that time is what Einstein made of it. While it is now known that the universe is expanding (radio waves taking billions of years to reach this planet tell us that clumps of matter are still being formed at the edges), it is not known what will be the future of this apparently limitless phenomenon, because it is not known how much matter will be in the universe in the remote future and how that will be affected by the force of gravity. Stars may multiply vastly but become weaker and weaker, so that finally they may be brought together in one graveyard, a singularity like the birthplace of the universe but currently going under a nickname as the 'Big Crunch'. However, it seems that a less romantic fate is more likely: the energy which has made the universe we know will burn out and matter will become dispersed radiation – in the 'Big Mist'.

What we do know is that every living creature must die as the price of life, and that all stars must also die since the nuclear process which makes them more than gas must eventually stop after becoming more intense in its last stages. And we know that the sun which makes life possible in this planet will eventually become too hot for life. Then it will become so fierce and large that it will absorb this planet.

Now that we know this, it is a relief to reflect that in striking contrast with the Utopian images in the apocalyptic literature of his people and period, there is no reliable evidence that Jesus ever indulged in fantasies about a physically glorious future for the world or for Israel in it. Passages in Scripture from other sources can be well known because beautiful, but on closer inspection they provide no information about the future, local or cosmic. An unknown prophet now called Second Isaiah predicted that the return of some Jews from exile in Babylon would be accompanied by the stupendous transformation of the wilderness and the countryside – but it was not. Another prophet who may be called Second John included in his Revelation vivid, but in detail incompatible, visions. For example, Earth is to be replaced by New Jerusalem, a city fifteen hundred miles broad and long, built with jewels and gold (21:15–21). He expected this to come quickly, but it did not. The poetry remains itself golden, but the message of the Bible taken as a whole seems more reliable as a guide: God will not die although everyone and everything will. After the natural death of this universe God may create another one, and many parallel universes may already exist with various characters, but such guesses cannot concern us greatly in the intervals between our own births and deaths. What can matter to us mortals is that the universe about which we can now begin to know something factual may be a waiting room, a place of inescapable decay and in the end of apparent futility, before 'the freedom of the glory of the children of God' whose home and school it briefly was (Romans 8:21).

That vision was developed by Paul or one of his disciples. The Ephesians were promised that in the fullness of time God's plan to gather up all 'things in heaven and things on earth' in Christ will be fulfilled (1:9, 10), and the Colossians were assured that already 'all things hang together' because in Christ they have been reconciled to God (1:17–20). On the surface this looks like a fantastic dream that the whole universe will be, or already is, one thing inside one man, but an interpretation of this imagery of mysticism may be offered. Their experience of Christ's power has become the most significant and revealing fact in the lives of Christians. It has led them to believe that the ultimate glory will be the bringing into God's eternity of the more-than-physical humanity which the creation of the physical universe made possible. And Christ is the foretaste, the first and already glorious model, of humankind, reconciled to God and capable of being united with 'all the fullness of God' (Ephesians 3:19) 'in the inheritance of the saints in the light' (Colossians 1:12).

It ought to be possible to restate the meaning of biblical visions of the universe, and of our destiny within it, in terms which take account of scientific knowledge, which itself must be for believers in some sense 'revelation' given by God. Ever since the Big Bang everything has flowed in one continuous stream, almost infinite in its immensity, variety, efficiency and beauty: there is no big gap between space and time, or between energy and matter, or between matter and life, or between any other form of life and us. As space expands it makes time; as energy is organised it becomes matter; as life evolves it becomes us. And this vision of cosmic unity, which is far more splendid than the old belief that the creation of everything as it is now took six days, does not contradict the belief that in deepest reality the natural processes of creativity from the one Source are sustained by the one Force, the Source and Force called God – the Reality within which the human animals who can be raised from the universal fate of mortality because of their capacity for mental and spiritual life will have a future transcending imagination.

However, although a faith may reckon with scientifically known facts and personally known experience, it can never be less or more than a faith, one interpretation of the facts which it fits. Faith is not strengthened in its true character by any claim that recent discoveries have provided fresh proofs of God's reality. As they push back the frontiers of human knowledge scientists are often in awe that their brains are able to take in so much that is new and strange. Their mathematics, producing equations which are simple, elegant and fruitful, seems to correspond with the structures of a very beautiful universe, and their logic and language seem more or less adequate to explain at least some of the mystery which would otherwise strip all pride from the human animals on this very tiny planet. Whether or not the word 'religion' is acceptable, such mathematics or science can be an intensely religious experience. But the science which uses the mathematics depends on precise observation, on coldly rational theories, and on the testing of theories by controlled and repeatable experiments, so that properly scientists do not think that it is within their professional competence to decide whether or not anything that exists has any purpose other than survival, preferably with usefulness and reproduction. The consideration of any such idea belongs to the debate about the merits of religious faith based on religious experience. What can be claimed with good reasoning is that during and since the 1960s new reasons have been supplied by science for not closing down that debate. As much as in the ages when it was believed that God had personally and rapidly made everything exactly as it is, it may be believed that the creation has a Creator.

Whether it is accepted or rejected, a religious faith is often thought to require the uncritical acceptance of a book, a creed or a longer collection of doctrines, because God has intervened to free some people from even the possibility of error. But that is clearly a mistake. No words can ever pin down the mysteries with which true religion deals. Words can help but they cannot be accurate reflections of the Infinite or perfectly clear echoes from the Eternal. Works of art can also help, but not even the greatest artist can paint or carve Reality. Music can help but even it depends on forged metal, the tusk of an elephant or the gut of an animal, or a human throat. This is because what true religion talks about is No-thing within, beneath and above everything.

Many people also like to think that faith in God must include the belief that 'he' frequently and reliably intervenes directly in events to help people for whom his love is special – but that is equally mistaken. The big fact is that in the main the development of this unimaginably large and old universe has been in regularities which can look like laws. Recently the fact has been established that the position and the momentum of anything smaller than an atom cannot be determined precisely and at the same time, so that it is for the observer to decide, if he so wishes, whether the thing looks like a particle or a wave. This 'uncertainty principle' has been used by some teachers of religion to claim that all science has lost any certainty and left the observer free to decide whether or not any event is an example of direct intervention by God – but that is not being serious about science or religion. Serious religion must try to account for the existence of things at least as big as atoms, which can be located and which when combined can be so orderly that things look solid. And serious science can stimulate thought about the true marvel: the outcome of the workings of nature are so often such that things can look as if they had been designed as they are.

Many very thoughtful scientists have therefore recently revived what in the eighteenth century was called 'Deism', the belief that apart from the creation the Creator is not noticeably active. But much religious, and all specifically Christian, experience suggests a faith which reaches beyond Deism into 'theism', the belief that God has a purpose and is still at work in order that it shall succeed. So the question arises: how does 'he' influence a creation which is, according to his own will, in general law-abiding? The best answer seems to be that in nature as a whole his activity is, by his own choice, hidden from us, so that we see only the outcomes. As we reflect about these results we may reasonably say that God 'lured' things in a good direction, or 'influenced' or 'guided' them if we think that stronger language is less inadequate. But that answer does not cover the religious experience of being more directly lured, influenced or guided by the God who is active because loving. So what more can we say?

Many people believe that God has intervened directly, repeatedly and sometimes dramatically in their lives, and since personal stories are useful here I may say that I can interpret my own life in that way. This includes times which I thought dark as necessary before times of joy. I believe I have been rescued and guided. But I find it impossible to think that in my life everything has been controlled by divine 'providence' for my sake and that nothing was caused either by regularity or by chance, both of which can seem to prevail in the creation outside me. I also know that I must never forget that many people throughout history have not been nearly so fortunate as I have been. So it would be wrong for me to claim certainty that any particular event which was to my benefit was directly and exclusively an act of God. I find it far easier to think that God can feed information and encouragement into a brain – even into mine – without adjusting the normal workings of nature and of history in order to suit my convenience. And that was why I was attracted to an interpretation of the resurrection of Jesus in which his 'appearances' were not physical miracles. Even there God kept his own rules (so to speak).

Many passages in the Bible reflect the belief, standard in the ancient world and still strong in traditional societies, that every event is caused directly, and controlled in detail, by God or by gods or other spirits, often for a particular purpose connected with humanity or a bit of it. But in a little-noticed deviation from that belief, Jesus is reported to have taught that 'your Father in heaven makes his sun to rise on the evil and on the good, and sends rain on the righteous and on the unrighteous' (Matthew 5:45). In other words, nature operates without any aim to bless or curse anyone; the sun and the rain have their own jobs to do in the Creator's plan. It is also said that when a falling tower has killed eighteen people the only religious lesson to be learned is that death comes to everyone and will be final unless people change their minds about life and God (Luke 13:4, 5). Such sayings may leave the impression that God was not believed by Jesus to be interested in individuals. However, it needs to be thought about in connection with the teaching that sparrows are captured, sold and eaten, yet not one of them is forgotten in God's sight – and that you who are 'of more value than many sparrows' have on your head hairs counted by the Creator of the universe (Luke 12:6, 7).

That last saying might leave a very different impression – that Jesus believed that unfailingly God protects both sparrows and people. But no one who seeks the truth can think that, and in particular no one who seeks to follow Jesus can forget how he died. However, he spoke also of the way in which, so to speak, the hairs on the head are counted finally. Even before he 'appeared' as alive after the torture of his death, he taught that after death the Father can show himself more clearly to be the God of individuals – of Abraham, Isaac and Jacob, but also of everyone. In another illuminating parable the Paradise enjoyed by Abraham opens to the beggar who had not been rescued from his plight before death; the dogs had been needed to lick his uncured sores. And the rich man from whom Lazarus had begged in vain, and who still wants the beggar to be sent out of Paradise as a messenger to a rich family, is after death 'tormented' by the results of his continuing self-centredness

(Luke 16:19–31). After death the mysteries of mortal life are over and the only remaining regularity is the direct rule of God. No interference with the 'laws' of nature is then necessary for the Father to show unmistakably that he cares about the individual. After what may be the agony of not knowing, 'then I shall know fully, even as I have been fully known' (1 Corinthians 13:12).

So the facts suggest that when asking about God's goodness we are asking about the One who is the sole origin of the only universe of which we have knowledge, but who works in a way which is not always clear and not always convenient to good people. That makes it necessary that eternal life should be possible and that teaching about it should be credible. It therefore needs to be taught plainly that it is the will of the Father that the whole of humankind should enter eternal life and it is not his will that anyone should be tortured endlessly in hell. Other doctrines have been taught by Christians but are increasingly seen to be morally indefensible. In the context of the whole teaching of Jesus it seems that, for example, the parable about the rich man being 'tormented' should now be understood as implying that any torments will cease if self-centredness is renounced. Then the Father, Abraham, Lazarus and the once-rich man will unite in joy. Selfishness is a road which, if taken to the end, will lead to the perdition which is death through complete self-destruction and that is the terrible truth – but if the eternal God is good, there must be an opportunity for a change of mind when his goodness is fully known after death and then 'there will be more joy in heaven over one sinner who repents than over ninety-nine righteous persons who need no repentance' (Luke 15:7).

It is also important to celebrate, not lament, the evident fact that God does not wield absolute power or have complete knowledge. If he did control everything he would be directly responsible for the many things in his creation, and in human lives in particular, which – we have to say – seem to have gone wrong. Even the happiest of us could, if also honest, make a long list of these. An all-powerful God could have prevented every one of them and an all-knowing God could have foreseen their disastrous consequences. Such a God should not be called 'good' if we use that term in the sense used when reacting to 'good' people – and no other sense seems to make sense. But we can in all honesty celebrate the goodness of God if we believe that he is responsible for a creation to which he has given a considerable degree of freedom, out of which has come the goodness we recognise. So far as we know, no other system was possible if this was to be the result.

He cannot be all-powerful ('omnipotent') or all-knowing ('omniscient') in every sense. We are able to do many things which God cannot do because he is infinite; for example, he cannot ride a bicycle. Nor can he do something which defies all the laws and logic in the creation: he cannot square a circle. And since it seems certain that there is an element of chance both in nature and history, and also that humans are to some extent free to make their own decisions, God cannot know everything which is going to occur before it occurs; for example, he cannot know for certain that at a particular juncture a particular cyclist will be damaged because a particular motorist has decided to drive dangerously.

It seems more sensible to ask what power and knowledge do belong to God. It seems logical to say that if 'he' is clever enough to create at least one universe, he is also able to know what is likely (not bound) to 'happen' and also what to do about it. Moreover, if he is such that we admire him he must be wise enough to have a policy of which the consequences are such that we, too, may rightly call them very good. So we have to ask what the consequences, taken together, are. Amid much that we cannot understand, we can draw on our own experience of pleasure in being creative to say that the Creator of everything must take delight in his achievement. That must be the main explanation of the scale of the creation, so staggering to us, so immense and so intricately beautiful in its details as in the picture as a whole. But what are the consequences for us? It seems undeniable that there is something that we must call chance, which means that some events must be out of control and that some of these will not be to our advantage. But it also seems that this element of chance is necessary if there is to be novelty, and that novelty is very much to our advantage – mainly because we are newcomers to the creation but also because we applaud many other late developments in the long, long story of evolution. And the freedom which has also made human life possible is its opportunity for glory. Up to a point we are free to decide what to be and to do, so that what we become in our struggles is authentically our own: we become fully ourselves, which may be a very good thing. And the greatest glory is that we can decide for ourselves whether or not to love our Creator in time or in eternity. For 'his' part the Creator can rejoice in that freedom, for the love we can give him can be free and therefore more precious than any behaviour which is compelled.

In this light it can be seen that despite all our limitations we are in some vital ways godlike because able to share the Creator's life, and up to a point that truth may be revealed to us by our own experience of creativity. Making anything begins in the pleasure we take in the material whose potentiality we can imagine. Shaping it adds to the pleasure. Finding the task unexpectedly difficult may end in the joy of defeating the problems. The material may seem to resist our efforts to make it conform to our initial vision, which may need some revision, but it all ends in the joy of work done. We have not changed essentially but we have gained, and the biggest gain may be an insight into the work of our Creator.

Even more relevant is our experience of parenthood. That begins in the joy of sex but greater pleasures follow the pain of childbirth, and the delight we can take in babies can be eclipsed by the joy of seeing adults able to decide for themselves to be what we have longed to see them be as they emerge out of the storms of adolescence. Even if having children brings us suffering or sorrow, we still do not regret having brought children into this imperfect world, because children can take and give love which is free.

What must be regarded as evil can be a part of the outcome of this divine or human way of creating or parenting, for wherever there is freedom there can be evil. But it seems reasonable to judge that the gains outweigh the losses. There is order which develops out of the chaos. There is beauty, seen as such in contrast with ugliness. There is goodness in contrast and conflict with evil. There is a courage which rises above evil and trusts that good will come out of it. And there is a compassionate wisdom which only one's own suffering under the iron rod of evil can make possible. So the question about God is not whether we should prefer him to have made more order, beauty, goodness and pleasure in the world around us; it is whether we are willing to link what actually exists with him. Of course there are many times when we find it difficult to believe that this is the best of all possible worlds, and we can offer complaints and suggestions. The question is whether there is enough good in the world we know to persuade us that the Source of it all is, in some sense which we cannot entirely understand, supremely rational, supremely beautiful and supremely good.

Again and again we shall have to tell ourselves not to make the decision to believe, or not to believe, on the basis of facts or experiences which are less than the whole in so far as this can be seen. One fact known to science must not be thought decisive, for or against God. One sunset must not convert us; one natural disaster must not make us atheists. One splendour in the mixture which is human must not bring us to our knees in adoration; one human failure or tragedy must not make us curse God. Believers must not pretend that a time of joy undeniably proves the goodness of God or that any bad experience must be a blessing in disguise, for it is always possible for others to say that something good is a mere accident and that something evil is sheer evil. It is on wider evidence that we can reasonably believe that the world in which we rejoice and suffer is indeed a creation, and that if at times the Creator may seem totally absent this is because he has to some

extent withdrawn from it in order to leave space for novelty through
freedom and ultimately for humans to decide to love in freedom.

This seems to be at least one way in which the decision between belief
and unbelief can be made in a time when the idea of God as a dictator
has been widely rejected for a host of reasons – and when even the
traditional idea of God as 'king' can be rejected by people who do not
remember that nowadays normally a monarch will have agreed to limit
the exercise of power. But it does not follow that God is more like a
family or a committee, involving three centres of consciousness,
thought and will.

Exponents of the 'social' version of the doctrine of the Holy Trinity
can claim that there must be three such centres in eternity because 'God
is love' and there cannot be love if there is only one 'person'. But it may
be asked what it means to say that 'God first loved us' (1 John 4:8) –
which all Christians would wish to say. This faith need not develop into
saying that God had to be plural long before there was any creature to
love. It did not so develop in the Johannine community: 'God's love was
revealed among us in this way: God sent his only son into the world . . .'
(4:9). If that is how divine love has been revealed, it seems that all that
is necessary for a Christian to believe is that in eternity God has always
had the desire and the capacity to love in 'his' own divine way. It may
help us to understand this mystery if we reflect that the average human
person has the desire and the capacity to become a true lover or parent
long before she or he ceases to be single.

It is the traditional orthodoxy of the Church, taught and defended
with a special passion in the Eastern Orthodox tradition, that the Father
is the sole source of divinity. Using human imagery, it is taught that the
Son was 'begotten' by him and that the Spirit 'proceeded' from him. But
Christians wanting simpler guidance know where to turn. It is firmly
the tradition set forth in the New Testament that when 'God sent his
Son', that Son would recite and quote 'The Lord is one. You shall love the
Lord your God with all your heart, with all your soul and with all your
might' (Deuteronomy 6:4,5) – and would teach that such love, respond-
ing to God, is enough to inspire the second essential commandment,
about love for the neighbour.

Some theologians have taught that relationships between humans,
and even between groups such as churches or nations, should be
modelled on the eternal 'communion' between the persons in the
Trinity. They have unintentionally made the urgently needed good relationships between individuals and groups even harder to achieve by
insisting that they should be based on the trinitarian mystery which
admittedly no one can fully understand. And they have expressed the

divine demand for better relationships in a way which is unrealistic. Human relationships must be strengthened and deepened by overcoming problems - but presumably there are no problems to be solved within the divine life. So it seems that from their lowly viewpoint the Trinity is best compared not with three connected pools but with a cascading waterfall.

What concerns us, practically and urgently, is the biblical message that we can have access to the eternal, all-holy and mysterious Father through the Son who shares our humanity and through the Spirit's gift of power to humankind. We hope to be united with God eternally, and meanwhile we can serve his rule over our world by doing his loving will. It is orthodoxy – again, stressed particularly in Eastern Orthodoxy – that our own life and work can be inspired by faith in the 'energies' of God at work, not by any full understanding of his eternal 'essence' or 'being'. It is not our duty to speculate about that; it is our duty to live in the light we have been given.

Least of all is it our duty to be precise about which is the work of which 'person' in the eternal Trinity. Paul was not precise. In the same passage (Romans 8:2–9) he could write about 'the Spirit of life in Christ Jesus', 'the Spirit of God' and 'the Spirit of Christ'. A great interpreter of Paul, Augustine of Hippo, found it more profitable to compare the Trinity with the memory, understanding and will of an individual, rather than with any society, however united. But he also taught eloquently that even calling God one person does not do justice to the richness of his divinity. And later teachers of the Church united in agreeing with the maxim that to us who are external to them, the operations of the Three are indivisible. Many modern theologians, among whom Barth and Rahner are perhaps the greatest names, have spoken of the Three as 'modes' of being God, God causing us and for us and near us – and that ought to be sufficient.

It has never been, and cannot be, orthodox to think that a Greek word translated as 'person' (through Tertullian's Latin *persona*) means what that word means in everyday English. The Father is not a man with a son but not much energy left, the Son is not a younger man with his own ideas, the Spirit is not someone so hard to identify that perhaps one is only imagining it as a distinct person, the three together are not a group which could be photographed, and it is wrong even to run the risk of leaving the impression that this is what one really thinks. What the Christian does think is that God has been revealed and experienced in three ways which are overwhelming influences, all equally divine. Yet these are not ways which can be separated. As revealed and experienced, the Father saves and inspires, the Son also creates and inspires, and the

Spirit is always at work in creation or salvation. Indeed, the power behind the Big Bang and all subsequent existence is the power behind all creativity, all salvation and all inspiration, anywhere. Our need is to receive this vast power into our lives day by day, not to attempt to carve it up into three people, and not to pretend to know about the home life of God.

The facts about evolution on this planet in the first two-thirds of its probable history strongly suggest that evolution is not over and may well include the step-by-step improvement of human bodies with their brains. In my own brief lifetime the technological advances devised in human brains have been staggering and there seems no likelihood that they will slow down. Much will depend on political leadership, but I have witnessed the birth of democracy on a global scale, at least as an ideal or a pretence, and it can seem possible that in the centuries to come the peoples of the world, having learned to speak up and being free to vote, will demand and obtain for all what 'ordinary' people have always wanted: peace, security, love in families, enough food, enough medicine and enough work and relaxation. If that future seems too good to be possible, we may take courage from faith in the Creator who will work to the end, and we can be cheered by some facts.

Since 1950 sport has not been the only sphere in which records have been broken. Although the world's population has doubled, so has the production of food. Never before has there been such international concern about the regional or local shortages which remain, or about natural disasters, or about international conflicts or civil wars which have caused massive but avoidable misery. Never before has an international institution been so effective as the United Nations, which admittedly is also defective. Never has racism been so condemned or concealed; never has imperialism aroused so little pride; never have such limits been placed on nationalism or tribalism; never have human rights been so widely enforceable by laws and justice; never have so many people been able to read and write; never since the developments of language and writing has there been an instrument of communication so full of promise (as well as danger) as the internet. In what is probably the most promising of all the changes which came in the twentieth century, never before have the rights of women been so widely acknowledged. Women have not ceased to be wives, mothers and homemakers but increasingly they control their own fertility and are free to have a life and do a worthwhile job outside the home. More often than before, the talents of the female half of humankind can be liberated from full-time, lifelong domesticity and exploitation in other workplaces – and the world has scarcely begun to see what gifts to its progress are being released.

Never before has the body housing the brain, female or male, been in a stronger position to go to work. In many countries life expectancy has increased dramatically, perhaps by a quarter of a century, because diseases which in the past brought premature death to almost everyone who had survived the perils of birth and infancy have been conquered. The very recent unravelling of many of the secrets of the body's genetic basis has opened up the possibility of medical progress pre-viously inconceivable. It remains a moral necessity to share existing and future medicine with the whole of humankind and the acceptance of that great task has begun. The plight of hungry and diseased children in Africa (for example) needs no emphasis here: the well-fed are already haunted by the images of despair brought into lounges by TV. It is already well known how easily curable in comparison are the problems of the privileged – obesity as their own symptom of malnutrition and a lack of physical exercise, and addiction to nicotine or another poisonous drug as a symptom of unwillingness to use the brain.

Brains freed from the drug of living-in-order-to-shop ought to be open to the fact that the one-third of humankind that is comparatively rich has enough wealth already for necessities and many luxuries, and thus is under an obligation to subsidise the development of the majority. In any respectable tradition of ethics, but particularly for Christians, this duty is undeniable. Not only do the less developed regions offer immense present dangers since poverty breeds disease and violence: they are also immense potential markets if free but fair trade could be secured. They are inhabited by most members of the human family, the best miracles in God's whole creation, and if the conscience of humankind is allowed to prevail a part of the kingdom of God will come on Earth, after all.

But it is an experienced fact that *Homo sapiens* is perfectly capable of rejecting both duty and opportunity, choosing instead both stupidity and sheer evil. In 1914–18 Europe did its utmost to commit suicide after building up such a system of alliances, supported by such large armies and navies, that both 'sides' felt themselves to be in mortal danger. In my own lifetime the stupidity of nations, which after the First World War had reduced Germany to poverty, stimulated the great evils of aggression and the Second World War. In its turn the war left both the West and the Soviet Union profoundly fearful and that very nearly stimulated the unspeakable great evil of the further use of nuclear weapons of mass destruction. When that danger receded it was slowly realised that the unchecked growth of the population in the poorer countries, and the unchecked growth of consumption in the richer, had raised the imminent danger that Earth would rebel against this new manifestation of human insanity. The soil would no longer grow enough food, enough drinkable water would no longer flow, nature would no longer supply enough raw material for the limitless appetite of modern manufacturing, the oceans would swallow much of the land and the air itself would be fouled. And the electronic revolution has raised the danger that the new means of communication will pollute the springs of imagination, accustoming humankind to habitual violence, mindless lust and pointless consumerism.

As I end this book it is doubtful whether *Homo sapiens* will have the imagination and the resolve either to 'make poverty history' (as now seems possible for the first time in history) or to 'save the planet' from the unprecedented but proved pollution of soil, water and air. It also seems possible that the saying will come true: Earth has cancer, and that cancer is us. Democracy can lead to the universal recognition of the basic rights of all humankind, but the selfish and short-sighted habits of electorates and elected politicians can also mean that the steps on which most experts agree, and which would carry a tolerable cost, will not be taken in time. One crucially important factor may be a decline in the belief that the creation has a Creator to whom we are answerable.

So it would be very foolish not to reckon with the folly and disaster which humans have often chosen and can choose again, in some cases encouraged by leaders commissioned to speak for religion and to guide morality. At the down-to-earth level at which Earth's future will be decided, I cannot avoid sharing the widespread conviction that a specially dangerous scandal is that the consecrated leaders of the largest of the Christian churches have not yet (2006) withdrawn their condemnation of the use of artificial contraceptives. To them this practice is against the laws of nature and therefore against the will of God. But in 1950 the population of Africa was approximately 200 million and, according to the United Nations, a projection based on the rates of fertility and mortality in 1950–2000 indicates that in 2050 the population will be about 1,600 million. The only alternative to death by starvation seems to be a limit imposed by the physical and mental agonies and the massacres inflicted by the condom-free pandemic of AIDS. Yet the dignity of *Homo sapiens*, fit to be called godlike, began in Africa.

In answer to such fears all that I have been able to present is this outline of a positive faith in God with the history of Jesus Christ at the centre. In that faith, if it could be stated worthily, the churches could, I believe, move beyond the current battles between conservatives and liberals and the current mixture of decline with precarious growth, and the world could find its best inspiration for a truly new age. But obviously the hope rests ultimately on what is believed to be the character of God as made known in his activity. If we are no longer to insist on the precise repetition of old doctrines, or to offer as the alternative nothing but doubts and denials, it must be because as a result of facts and experiences we have been gripped by a vision of the God who is not only old and not only new. So I submit my own creed:

> God is greater and better than we can imagine
> but he is rightly pictured as creator, father, mother.
> He is essential to all that exists,
> he is eternal while everything dies.
> All beauty comes from his beauty,
> all health from his activity,
> all goodness from his holiness,
> all order from what he orders,
> all truth from what he reveals.
> He ardently loves his whole creation,
> he has given it a large freedom to make itself,
> he rejoices that the outcome is so good,
> he delights in it and suffers with it,
> and we are his masterpieces
> meant to be as eternal as he is,
> but he has made us free to reject him.
> He has spoken through many prophets and
> his love is embodied uniquely and supremely in Jesus,
> human, crucified and triumphant,
> Teacher, Saviour and Lord.
> His power is poured out as his Spirit inspires
> all who follow Jesus and
> all who follow the light they see.
> In and beyond any tragedy he can save:
> any human failure can be redeemed,
> he can guide us to rescue Earth,
> he can make us fit to share his own home.
> Everyone who asks will be answered by God,
> everyone who seeks will find God,
> everyone who loves will be loved
> and held for ever in God's love.
> Before death what we can do is to love God
> as much as heart, soul, mind and body can,
> and therefore love all the creation.
> For Christians this is the right conservatism
> and the right liberalism is liberation

where anything is less than true,
where anyone is less than free,
where life is not richly abundant,
where evil resists God's plan which is government by love.

INDEX